BY THE SWEAT OF THY BROW
Work in the Western World

Books by Melvin Kranzbeg

TECHNOLOGY IN WESTERN CIVILIZATION
(CO-EDITED WITH CARROLL PURSELL)

TECHNOLOGY AND CULTURE
(CO-EDITED WITH WILLIAM H. DAVENPORT)

Books by Joseph Gries

BRIDGES AND MEN

ADVENTURE UNDERGROUND

LIFE IN A MEDIEVAL CITY
(CO-AUTHORED WITH FRANCES GRIES)

MERCHANTS AND MONEYMEN
(CO-AUTHORED WITH FRANCES GRIES)

BY THE SWEAT OF THY BROW

Work in the Western World

by MELVIN KRANZBERG
and JOSEPH GIES

G. P. Putnam's Sons, New York
Capricorn Books, New York

1164151

Contents

II. WORK IN THE EARLY INDUSTRIAL AGE

III. MODERN PRODUCTION: TECHNOLOGY AND CONSEQUENCES

Introduction

1. Work and Workers: From Production Goals to Self-Fulfillment

An intriguing discovery made by anthropologists who have studied surviving "primitive" societies in the Arctic, Africa, and elsewhere is the absence among these people of a word for work. Yet their vocabularies are extraordinarily rich in terms for all aspects of hunting, fishing, and other life-sustaining activities. Eskimos, for example, have more than twenty words for snow, and different words for the same animal in different states relevant to hunting —"walking-bear," "sleeping-bear," "dangerous-bear."[1]

The explanation of this linguistic paradox, the anthropologists have concluded, is simply that among such subsistence groups work is so synonymous with living and breathing that no word is needed for it. On their economic level one does not distinguish between working and not working, but only between waking and sleeping, because to be awake means to be working.

For some two million years—virtually the whole of our species' existence—the life of all mankind, except in a few favored locations and times, consisted mostly of work.[2] Man was born, he worked, and he died.[3]

What at long last broke this interminable human routine was the invention of the division of labor, or the organization of work. From simple beginnings—the partition of tasks between men and women or between old and young—the organization of work developed complexity with an astonishing speed. In a few thousand years, a mere few dozen generations, it ramified into modern industrial society, with its 25,000 different full-time occupations, each of which defines its practitioner in terms of income, education, social status, living standard, life-style.

The dynamism of the history of work organization, especially in the Western countries, has had a ceaseless impact on the whole of society, repeatedly shaking it to its foundations. Yet intellectual perception lagged far behind, and only very slowly did thinkers awaken to the immense significance of how the work force is organized to perform its tasks. Not till late in the nineteenth century did some of the implications begin to draw attention. The observation of the phenomenon of interdependence—the individual worker performing a limited function and relying on many other workers elsewhere in the production apparatus to supply his needs—became an important element in the foundation of sociology.

The Victorian intellectual Herbert Spencer, sometimes thought of as the father of sociology, made the significant assertion that a society can only be said to exist when cooperation is present among a group of individuals.[4] Another founder of the new discipline, Emile Durkheim, in his classic work *The Division of Labor in Society (De la Division du Travail Social)* laid emphasis on the specialization of function in human society:

> It can even be said that the more specialized the functions of the organism, the greater its development. . . . [It] is a phenomenon of general biology whose conditions must be sought in the essential properties of organized matter. The division of labor in society appears to be no more than a particular form of this general process; and societies, in conforming to that law, seem to be yielding to a movement that was born before them, and that similarly governs the entire world.[5]

The organization of work, embodying the principles of specialization of function and division of labor, Durkheim identified as an explanation alike of biological evolution and societal development, in keeping with the contemporary fashion of applying Darwin's discoveries to social theory. Despite this uncritical approach likening the social organism directly to evolutionary biology, Durkheim broke important new ground in recognizing the social significance of occupations. On the one hand he perceived the interdependence created by modern society's proliferation of occupational functions as a cement binding society together, to some extent even taking the place of religion as a unifying element in civilization. But on the other hand Durkheim detected a danger that the division of labor might become so complex that the individual would no longer see his own role as integrated with that of others, that he would become psychologically disconnected and lost, feeling his life to be meaningless. To this potential malady Durkheim gave the name "anomie." For anomie to be avoided, Durkheim thought, the worker must not "lose sight of his collaborators," he must be conscious of the fact "that he acts upon them and reacts to them."

Durkheim's pioneering work has been followed up by many twentieth-century thinkers who to Durkheim's anomie have added such terms as "alienation" and "identity crisis." Other social scientists have turned their attention to the relationship between tools and production techniques on the one hand and the organizational aspects of work on the other. It is evident enough that changes in technology can bring changes in the way work is organized. Hand tools mean hand craftsmanship, powered machinery suggests the factory, computers and transfer machines imply automation. Even within this concept there are many subtleties not at once visible and certainly difficult to anticipate in advance, such as the complex effects of automation, but the general principle has long been familiar. What is less readily discernible is that the relationship between technology and the organization of work is a two-way street. "Work, its structure, organization, and concepts," Peter Drucker has written (in *Technology and Culture*), "must in turn powerfully affect the tools and techniques and their development."[6]

A surprising and to some observers upsetting discovery of recent years has been the fact that as the number of highly industrialized nations has increased, new and different ways of organizing the same kind of technically advanced production have appeared. Work, it seems, can be organized quite differently in different countries (or even sometimes inside the same country) for the production of the same product on the same machines. Differing traditions, government and labor-union rules, varying approaches to the work process by the workers, bring different rates of productivity in automobile factories in the United States and abroad, even factories owned by the same company and producing nearly identical automobiles on similar assembly lines. The phenomenon runs counter to the "convergence" theory of Soviet physicist Andrei D. Sakharov and others who have postulated the eventual disappearance of the differences in Soviet and American societies through the operation of similar industrial processes.

The mutuality of the interrelationship between tools and work organization is well established, but by no means completely understood. It is not difficult to see how the introduction of mechanized, power-driven spinning processes in eighteenth-century England altered traditional domestic work organization in the manufacture of textiles. It is less easy to see how different patterns for the organization of work affected the productivity of spinning machines at different times, places, and situations, yet this has been the case.

Similarly, Adam Smith's dictum[7] that "the division of labor is limited by the extent of the market" is more self-evident than the later corollary, that the extent of the market is limited by the degree of the division of labor. As the division within each producing community fractionated through the course of the nineteenth century, the division among different communities in the same country and among the countries of the world also increased, and with the heightened fragmentation of producers, all more and more in need of goods produced elsewhere, came a steadily expanding world market.

By the end of the nineteenth century it was accepted as axiomatic that a systematic breakdown of jobs into their components diminished costs and increased output. The twentieth century brought a slow awakening to the fact that this truism is not always true. Workers limited to a single undemanding task become bored and produce less, or produce less meticulously. The discovery of this phenomenon has led to a profound change in industrial-management concepts. Where for a century and more it was taken for granted that the direction of advance in industrial efficiency lay entirely in the realm of technology, that is, through increasing the number and enhancing the design of machines and optimizing their organizational pattern, the worker himself suddenly emerged as a paramount consideration.

The first man to perceive the importance of the individual worker in factory production was Frederick Winslow Taylor, whose remarkable insights in the 1880's and 1890's led to a revolution in industrial technique. But brilliant and original though Taylor's ideas were, they were fatally compromised by the limitations of Taylor's background as an industrial engineer, which blinded him to the complex shape of the worker's relationship to his work. That perception began to develop with the research of Elton Mayo and his successors in the 1920's and 1930's, when the behavioral sciences at last began taking their place on the industrial scene alongside the physical and engineering sciences. The human needs of the worker were at last recognized as broader than the purely material wants that Taylor took into consideration. Adam Smith's picture of Economic Man and Frederick Winslow Taylor's picture of Mechanical Man were gradually fleshed out to the breadth and stature of a real-life organism with characteristic social and psychological needs—a process not yet completed.

Meantime, the continuing progress of technology and the organization of work were bringing onto the horizon a surplus of material goods. As social welfare advanced thanks to this growing surplus, the possibility loomed of assuring the basic necessities for all, at least in the advanced countries. What might be called the "nonwork movement" made its appearance in the 1960's, composed of young people who felt no imperative need to achieve traditional work goals and who worked, if at all, at "doing their thing," typically some form of craftsmanship. This development was possible only because of our technological society's ability to produce a sufficiency of material goods and creature comforts for all. That in turn fortified the tendency to endow work with larger goals, non-material as well as material—the quality of life, self-esteem, basic satisfaction on the part of the worker with his human condition. A significant new element in labor negotiations of the 1970's has been summarized in the phrase, "They used to want more pay, now they want more say."

As skills have increasingly been built into the machine, and as the worker has changed from a craftsman to a machine operator to a machine overseer, the organization of work has had to respond to the changes in technology. That was not all. It further developed that the technology in turn had to respond to the human needs of the worker. Industrial management must address itself to the whole man-machine interface. The problem, in all its complexity, is not limited to the factory; it exists also in agriculture and the other economic sectors.

A host of special problems have arisen in the United

States and abroad as the industrial labor force augments at the same time that it changes its character and composition. In America the entry of women and blacks into the job market in areas and on levels where they were previously excluded has required fresh examination of work organization and technology. The cultural deprivation of black and other minority workers means that many jobs must be redesigned to allow for a lower educational level on the part of the operator, while the lesser physical strength of women often requires similar technological and organizational adjustment.

Nor is it simply the factory that is affected by the continuous change in work patterns. The working force includes not only the blue-collar worker but the teacher, the office worker, the computer programmer. The whole area of health services is being radically affected by the introduction of paramedical personnel, bringing a new division of labor never before experienced in the medical profession. The computer has had a similarly dramatic impact on clerical and white-collar work in thousands of offices.

Technological change will remain with us. Far from slowing down it even appears to be accelerating, along with its interacting partner, the organization of work. As new changes come in work patterns new social needs will inevitably be felt that will in turn have their own impact on the whole economic process.

The future is never foreseeable, but it is a measure of defense to expect the unexpected. One method of preparation is to examine the path that led us to where we are, the steps our forebears took in their increasingly swift plunge toward what to them was a totally unforeseeable future.

I. Work in the Pre-Industrial Age

2. The First Divisions
of Labor:
Age, Sex, Craft

The division of labor is probably as old as *Homo sapiens*, and may in fact antedate the appearance of our human species. Indeed, the organization of work through division of labor may have played a role, along with tools, a more complex brain structure, and language communication, in differentiating man from other animal species.

In the earliest stage of human development, lasting through the eons of prehistory known as the Old Stone (Paleolithic) Age, from somewhere between 2,000,000 and 1,000,000 B.C. to 10,000-8,000 B.C., allocation of work was virtually confined to food gathering. Scattered in isolated groups, the earth's tiny population ranged forests and prairies, hunting, fishing, rooting, and berrying, in an unceasing struggle to escape starvation. Lack of communica-

13

tion among groups as well as the scantiness of food surpluses limited geographical division of labor, though those
living along rivers or on the seacoast doubtless specialized
in fishing, and others in hunting certain animals. Each
group's food-gathering activities, however, required organization within the group.[1]

The most obvious source of division of labor arose from
the differences of age and sex. Old people lacking the
strength and agility for hunting and foraging were given
sedentary tasks, such as food preparation, while children
were started on their lifelong food-gathering careers by
training in collecting nuts and berries. In early societies
there could be no idlers; the food supply was too precari-
ous, and children began doing their share as soon as they
were able.

The sexual division of labor derived from woman's
childbearing and child-nursing role. A pregnant woman or
a nursing mother—and most women were one or the other
most of the time—could not participate effectively in the
hunt, which was restricted to men. This consideration did
not prevent women from being accorded an equal share of
physical labor, or even the larger share. It has been said that
woman is man's oldest beast of burden, an arrangement
that may reflect the community's dependence on man's
hunting weapons for defense, implying a need to leave the
man relatively unencumbered, for example during a move
from one hunting or foraging ground to another. Interestingly, skeletal comparisons reveal fewer morphological differences between men and women of prehistoric times than
do those of today, suggesting a more equal division of heavy
labor than in more recent times.

Our knowledge of the earliest human communities dis-
closes no evidence of class distinctions, indicating an ab-

sence of a nonsexual division of labor. Although recent studies have shown that some hunting-foraging societies were reasonably well fed, or at least did not live constantly on the edge of famine,[2] nobody could be spared for non-food tasks. There were no warrior or priestly aristocracies, and no full-time specialists. There were, however, part-time specialists. Male hunters had always doubtless made their own snares and hunting weapons, while women made their own implements. When hunters learned to use flint tools and weapons, some inevitably proved especially skilled at knapping, or chipping, flint. These experts produced more arrowheads and knife blades than they could themselves use, and traded them for food captured by the most proficient hunters and fishermen. Available evidence on the flint-knappers of the New Stone (Neolithic) Age nowhere suggests that these men confined themselves to making tools and weapons; they also used their own products to hunt food themselves.

Besides the division of labor implied by the part-time specialists, the hunting societies of the Stone Age required a form of work organization in the food-gathering activity itself.[3] Hunting small game and fishing could be carried on by individuals without any significant cooperation, but hunting large animals demanded a coordinated group activity, typically luring herds of wild animals and driving them toward hunters lying in ambush. Bones of large animals killed by hunters have been found in Upper (later) Paleolithic sites dating as far back as 40,000 B.C. Implied in the hunt organization are leaders to plan and organize the sharing of the kill among participating groups. Thus hunting, especially of large animals, begins the long evolution of planning and group action. Also implied is a shift in the level of group self-sufficiency from the single family to a considerably larger (though perhaps kinship-based) grouping.

The natural division of labor between male hunters and female and child food gatherers was accentuated by the development of large hunting groups. The division, however, was neither absolute nor continuous. Hunting in its nature tends to be part-time and seasonal, so that the hunters often joined the women and children in searching for plant food. Recent studies have shown, contrary to what was long believed, that the foraging side of the hunting-foraging society usually provided the larger share of the food.[4]

Domestication of animals began in the Upper Paleolithic with the hunting dog. At roughly the same time that man was passing on some of the most arduous work of hunting—tracking the quarry—to his new non-human assistant, he was himself creating the first expressions of his distinctively human aesthetic instinct in the cave paintings of southern France and Spain and the Ural Mountains of the Soviet Union. When these were first discovered it seemed incredible that they were actually the work of "primitive" man, so graceful and realistic were the representations of animals and hunters. When it was conclusively demonstrated that these paintings dated to Paleolithic times their artistic merit led art critics to conclude that they were done by a special class of trained artists, but anthropologists find no evidence of this. The most probable assumption is that the cave painters, like the flint-knappers, were part-time specialists. It is also possible that the work was part of the ritual of the hunt, with the paintings or the act of painting believed to confer hunting prowess.

A possible very early division of labor about which we can

only conjecture is that implied by early man's fire-keeping. The French structural anthropologist Claude Lévi-Strauss, in *The Raw and the Cooked*, expresses the view that one dividing line between "nature" and "culture" is the application of fire to food,[5] and there is little doubt that once men had tasted cooked meat they tried hard to keep their fires alive. Man, it should be noted, possessed fire long before he mastered the means of kindling it. When a fortuitous stroke of lightning provided a blaze, it might well have been deemed worthwhile to assign people—probably women and children—to collecting twigs and branches to keep it going.

The first unmistakable evidence of a higher order of work organization than that involved in the hunt comes from pottery-making. Clay is more or less universally distributed, but the best raw material for ceramics is scattered randomly, leading to geographical specialization in pottery-making and commerce in the products. The earliest potters were doubtless part-time food gatherers, and later part-time agriculturists, and it is by no means certain, as has often been stated, that pottery-making was carried on by women in early societies. Nevertheless, there is reason to believe that some kind of work organization was involved in even early ceramic production.[6] Digging and firing may have been the work of men, while the fashioning and decorating was done by women. The step-by-step character of the work would seem to dictate the first appearance of the attempt to rationalize production into specialized tasks.

The same kind of specialization may be assumed in the earliest textile manufacture. The need for cloth arose with the Neolithic substitution of agriculture for hunting, and consequent reduction in the supply of animal skins, hitherto the major source of garments. Textiles required a spinning process, the earliest tools for which were the spindle and distaff. The traditional association of women with the distaff may indicate a sexual division of labor, with the man turning the spindle while the woman held the distaff, a forked stick on which the unspun fibers were hung.[7]

Early agriculture may also have made use of an organization of work along sexual lines, the women, perhaps assisted by children, planting and cultivating while the men hunted. Ancient mythology possibly lends credence to the assumption of women as agriculturists; Isis, Cybele, Demeter, and Ceres, the Egyptian, Asian, Greek, and Roman divinities of grain-raising are all goddesses. More probably, however, the goddess seemed appropriate as a symbol of fertility. Men undoubtedly participated from the beginning in some agricultural tasks, such as clearing the land. In the Neolithic communities that grew up in the Near East about 10,000 B.C., where agriculture first began to assert its superiority to hunting as a source of food, the evidence suggests that the men rather than the women tilled the soil.

The revolution by which agriculture displaced hunting and gathering required some thousands of years, a progress in work organization that by comparison with the million to two million years of the Old Stone Age is headlong. Two distinct types of agriculture developed: herding and crop farming. The former was characterized by "transhumance," the seasonal migration to follow the grassland flowering. The latter, with its sedentary life, favored the development of more complex forms of society.

Even in its earlier stages agricultural production seems to have provided a slight surplus that was capable of supporting a class of specialists of decisive importance: makers of metal tools and weapons. From metallurgy derive the full-time specialists and the higher level of work organization of civilized societies.[8]

The first full-time specialist was probably a metalworker. The origins of metallurgy remain shrouded, but the growing use of metal for tools and weapons in the Neolithic Age (roughly 8000 to 3000 B.C.) unmistakably points to the evolution of a class of full-time miners and artisans. Prospecting, mining, and smelting copper ore, and tool and weapon fabrication required a degree of skill and strength that militated against any but full-time specialists, making it necessary for even the earliest metalworkers and their families to be supported by surplus foodstuffs produced by farming communities and exchanged for metal tools, utensils, and weapons. The oldest known metallurgical sites lie in areas not far from the irrigation-farming valleys of the Nile, the Tigris-Euphrates, and the Indus rivers that are capable of providing a high yield per acre.[9] Even in these fertile regions the Neolithic surpluses were small, but because the areas were large enough to sustain sizable farming populations, the total agglomeration sufficed to support small classes of full-time specialists. When early copper sites lay in mountainous regions where climate and topography made agriculture difficult or impossible, the ore-rich veins could only be exploited by organizing long-distance transport, eventually necessitating the development of specialist classes of traders and transport workers.

Besides metalworkers, the early specialist classes included luxury-goods workers and priests. These latter, specialists in "magic," including the knowledge of mathematics and astronomy, may well have appeared on the scene ahead of the metallurgists, but have left no artifacts to prove it.

There is some evidence that whole villages or tribes may have specialized in metallurgy. In parts of Arabia and Africa today certain tribes circulate among the farmers and herdsmen as tinkers and metalworkers.[10] Certainly one effect of metallurgical development was the rise of classes of traders and transporters, since copper ore and copper products had to be moved over long distances.

The existence of a class of metalworkers itself stimulated the formation of other crafts. Neolithic farmers dug their own flint, made their own tools and weapons, spun their own thread to weave their own cloth, and made their own footwear and pots. The new group of metalworkers lacked the time to supply themselves with these necessities, just as they lacked the time to raise their own food, so that a tendency developed for part-time or full-time specialization in clothmaking, shoemaking, and pottery-making, crafts that would also supply their products to the new classes of priests and nobles (warriors).

The basic complexity of metalworking as contrasted with flint working had the further effect of creating subdivisions of labor. When the first sources of copper ore, the outcroppings, were exhausted, mining techniques had to be devised (at first little different from those used by earlier flint miners). Separation of metal from the ore required specialized knowledge. So did the casting and forging processes by which the smith transformed the lumps of metal into implements, finishing them by hammering, shaping, grinding, and polishing. At an early date the value of alloying copper with tin or zinc to produce bronze or brass, with enhanced hardness and toughness, was discovered, further heightening the degree of specialized knowledge and skill needed in metallurgy.[11]

The combination of agricultural surpluses and copper-based tools provided the technical foundation for the great irrigation civilizations that rose in the Near, Middle, and Far East by about 3000 B.C. In these civilizations the organization of work developed along lines that in their principal aspects remained unchanged for the next 5,000 years, that is, until the arrival of industrial machine power in the eighteenth century.

3. Irrigation and Classes: Theories of Civilization and Society

The most striking feature of the river valley civilizations that grew up in Mesopotamia and Egypt (as well as in China and India) is their large-scale irrigation systems. So impressed was the German scholar Karl Wittfogel with these great works that in his seminal study *Oriental Despotism* (1957) he expressed the conviction that the organizational hierarchies of the ancient kingdoms of the Near East stemmed directly from the need for coordination and direction of construction on the irrigation systems.

"If irrigation farming depends on the handling of a major supply of water . . . a large quantity of water can be channeled and kept inbounds only by the use of mass labor," he wrote, "and this mass labor must be coordinated, disciplined, and led."[1] Therefore, according to Wittfogel, a class of leaders arose wielding political power, forming the first true governments of states. The tribal leadership of earlier societies represented only a personal type of government, usually exercised by a patriarch over a kinship group. Now for the first time an impersonal government was established and institutionalized in the form of a permanent bureaucratic hierarchy.

The impact of the new irrigation systems on the food supply had momentous consequences not only on the division of labor but on the structure of society itself. The new food surpluses went to support not only specialized craftsmen—smiths, potters, weavers—but merchants who dealt in the new surplus commodities. As villages grew into towns and cities many other occupations and professions proliferated. Two of especial significance were the warriors and the priests. In the old communal hunting and gathering society, the hunters had themselves provided the defense force, but in the new farming communities the immobile and vulnerable farm families had to be protected by a special military organization. At the same time the old tribal dieties, no longer appropriate in a detribalized society, gave way to regional and city gods, whose more sophisticated cults required the services of a new educated class. Army and clergy helped weld towns, cities, and farms into kingdoms or empires. Typically, the monarch himself, such as the Egyptian pharaoh, assumed the trappings of deity.

Though Wittfogel's irrigation thesis may help explain the social revolution of the fourth millennium B.C., its application must be limited at least to the great river basin civilizations of the Tigris-Euphrates, the Nile, the Indus, and the Hwang-Ho valleys. More recent scholars have cast doubt on its universal validity, pointing out that urban civilizations emerged elsewhere without, or previous to, large-scale irrigation works.[2] Other factors—geographical features, natural resources, climate, plants and animals susceptible of domestication, relations with neighboring peoples—are often discernible in the growth of social organisms. Some years before Wittfogel, British anthropologist Gordon Childe[3] had pointed to the dramatic effects of Neolithic agricultural surpluses in freeing some of the group from primary food production to become potters, weavers, and smiths, and traced the development of political integration simply to the growing complexity of the economic society resulting from such division of labor. Other scholars, notably Franz Oppenheimer,[4] have seen the conquest of agriculturists by pastoral nomads as the decisive event in creating the state. Robert L. Carneiro has recently advanced "A Theory of the Origin of the State" that he calls "environmental circumscription."[5] In areas of "circumscribed" farmland, Carneiro suggests, such as the Nile, the Tigris-Euphrates, or the Indus valley, or the valleys of Mexico and Peru, geographical obstacles such as mountains, seas, and deserts may so limit arable land that a growing population may create an incentive to conquest. Resulting war, according to this theory, creates a new class structure with an upper warrior class and a lower servile class of war captives.

The classic Marxist interpretation[6] has long pictured a class structure arising from the exploitation of the weaker members of a society by the more powerful. A few farmers who were especially lucky or successful in crop raising could acquire surpluses they could barter for tools, with which they could still further improve on their production, perhaps permitting them to acquire weapons that gave them power over their neighbors.

Though we have very insufficient knowledge of the

structure of prehistoric society, it is generally believed that the hunters and food gatherers of the Old Stone Age lived in a communist economic state, with wealth considered the property of the tribe or community and with the welfare of each individual regarded as the responsibility of the group. The change from hunting to agriculture could hardly fail to shatter the basis of this communist society by permitting the single farming family to become a self-sufficient unit and inevitably creating class differences through the uneven accumulation of surpluses. Whatever the exact sequence—nomadic warriors taking over from sedentary villagers, or semi-agricultural warriors organizing super-villages that evolved into states—what is certain is that the old village autonomy was transcended by a larger socio-economic unit that became the nucleus of the new larger political unit.

Whatever the details of the "Neolithic Revolution," in Gordon Childe's famous phrase, it had by 3000 B.C. transformed the egalitarian communities of the earlier Stone Age, in the advanced food-producing regions, to totally different social structures. In these the masses of the people were reduced to servile status and kept economically at subsistence level by the systematic expropriation of their surplus production for the benefit of a small class of kings, noble warriors, and priests, and to support the army and the bureaucracy (whose chief function was tax collecting, in other words, expropriating the surpluses). Class division, representing a division of labor, thus became the foundation of the social structure. As the elite groups at the top continued to concentrate wealth in their own hands they inspired still more specialists to come into existence to serve their increasingly sophisticated needs. Besides potters, weavers, armorers, and metalworkers, there now appeared clerks or scribes, possessing the mysterious arts of writing and mathematics. In the irrigation civilizations the large agricultural surpluses called into being a class of merchants, in whose train lawyers and other auxiliaries of commerce followed.

By the time prehistory gives way to history—by the time written records appear—the social structure had become a pyramid at whose apex stood the ruler and the nobles, with whom the priests were closely aligned. In Mesopotamia the priests served as the bureaucracy and directed the economy. Both Mesopotamia and Egypt had nationalized economies in which the state owned the land and virtually all its products. In Mesopotamia the economic system operated through the priests' temples, and in Egypt through the civil bureaucracy of the Pharaoh. In Mesopotamia the peasants brought their taxes, in the form of harvested grain, to the Temple storehouse, where it was tallied by the priests. In Egypt the same record-keeping function devolved on the Pharaoh's clerks.

While the mass of the people were peasants and craftsmen, these two classes did not form the lowest order of the social scale. That belonged to the class of slaves. Originating either as captives of war or as debtors, the slaves performed the most arduous tasks, such as serving in construction gangs and working in underground mines. Above the peasants and craftsmen were the merchants and the professionals—doctors, lawyers, judges, scribes—and above these the dual ruling class of warriors and priests. The social structure of the early despotisms of Mesopotamia and Egypt was carried over into classical Greece and Rome. For relatively brief periods in both Greece and Rome, republican or democratic governments succeeded in doing away with the old ruling elite and substituting the class of free landholding peasants, doubling as warriors, as the governing organism of society.

Nevertheless, the basic organization of work remained unchanged: a pyramid with a ruling elite at the top and slaves at the bottom, and a growing number of crafts and trades in between, with peasant agriculturalists forming the bulk.

A characteristic of the ancient world that drew perhaps exaggerated attention of later ages was the low opinion held of manual labor. In Homeric times (ninth century B.C.) Odysseus and Penelope suffered no demeaning effects from manual labor, the hero caring for his own cattle and his wife doing her own weaving. But by the Athenian Golden Age attitudes had changed. Plato distinguished between work of the hand and work of the mind in decided favor of the latter, and Xenophon in his *Oeconomicus* has Socrates speak as follows:

> What are called the mechanical arts carry a social stigma and are rightly dishonored in our cities. For these arts can damage the bodies of those who work at them or who act as overseers, by compelling them to a sedentary life and to an indoor life, and in some cases, to spend a whole day by the fire. This physical degeneration results also in deterioration of the soul. Furthermore, the workers at these trades simply have not got the time to perform the offices of friendship or citizenship. Consequently they are looked upon as bad friends and bad patriots, and in some cities, especially the warlike ones, it is not legal for a citizen to ply a mechanical trade.[7]

Socrates', or Xenophon's, greatest scorn is clearly directed at the metallurgical trades, as witness his derogation of spending the day by the fire. In Greek mythology the god of metallurgy was Hephaestus, who alone among the gods had a physical imperfection, a limp that gave further credence to the belief that the manual arts deformed the body. Hephaestus was also the butt of jokes among his fellow Olympians, whose social attitudes reflected those of ancient Hellas. Aristotle felt that leisure was essential "both for growth in goodness and for the pursuit of political activities," and that work, as an obstacle to such fulfillment, was degrading.[8] A few centuries later, Plutarch (c. A.D. 46-120), recalling the Age of Pericles, thought no wellborn young man would even want to be Phidias, because a sculptor uses tools and gets covered with dust and sweat.[9]

Yet there is evidence that certain kinds of work were respected. Labor on the land did not incur the same contempt as the work of craftsmen and traders. Cicero pointed out that life in the fields strengthened body and soul, and that love for the soil was an important ingredient of patriotism.[10] A modern view is that the ancient world did not regard manual labor in itself as degrading, but rather the ties of dependence created by working for others in return for payment.[11] It was not considered demeaning to build one's own house or ship, as did Odysseus, or to spin and weave one's own cloth, as did Penelope. It was the idea of being dependent on someone else for wages that was regarded as shameful. Artisans who sold their products or hired out their services could not be regarded as truly free. For this reason the artisan was distinguished from the freeholding peasant and held in less esteem.

The universal institution of slavery undoubtedly operated to heighten contempt for manual labor, yet it is worth noting that in the classical world slaves were not segregated.

In both Greece and Rome free men and slaves labored side by side in fields and workshops and on the great public works.

At least as significant as the denigration of manual labor (an attitude not completely corrected in later ages[12]) was the recognition of the social importance of the division of labor. In his *Republic* Plato asserted that the happy state, like the happy individual, is the one in which each part of its being is performing its proper function. "More is done, and done better and more easily," he asserted, "when one man does one thing according to his capacity and at the right moment." And in his *Laws*, Plato specified, "Let no ironworker work in wood; let no wood-worker have iron-workers under him; let each practice one single trade, by which he will live." He further recommended that each city should produce what it could best make, and exchange it with other cities for their own special products. That Plato's discussion of economics did not take place in a vacuum may be seen in the speech attributed to Pericles describing the work on the Acropolis;

All kinds of raw materials, marble, brass, ivory, gold, ebony, cypress, have been put in hand by craftsmen of all classes, carpenters, moulders, bronze-workers, marble-workers, goldsmiths, turners, painters, enamelers, and metalchasers. For carriage we have needed merchants, sailors, and pilots on the sea, and on land cartwrights, ox-drivers, waggoners, rope-makers, sail-makers, leather-dressers, road-menders and miners. And every trade . . . enjoys an ordered crowd of workers and an organized body of labor.[13]

Thus the classical Western world achieved a high and in

many ways efficient division of labor in an urban civilization characterized by a multitude of crafts and professions, structured into a hierarchical society dominated by a ruling elite, and including classes of merchants, who often acquired great wealth and power.

At the bottom was the large class of slaves, whose significance in the development of the classical civilization goes beyond their immediate economic importance. The slaves relieved the citizen class of time-and-energy-consuming tasks and permitted them to spend time in philosophical pursuits, athletic events, and the fine arts. But slaves also inhibited the development of technology.[14] Lacking power machinery and labor-saving devices, the Greek and Roman economies perforce relied on their "capital of flesh and working plant of muscle" for all major enterprises, such as bridge, road, aqueduct, and temple building, and the reliance, together with the availability of slaves (mainly through wars and conquest), removed the incentive for improving technology. Slavery became, as one illuminating phrase has it, "a lazy solution to technical problems." It might be pointed out too that slaves are by no means necessarily incapable of invention, but that the condition of slavery does not encourage it because no matter how much a slave might improve the efficiency of the operation he was engaged in, he would still be a slave, working just as hard and long as ever.

At the opposite end of Greek society the ivory-tower intellectuals were capable of brilliant mechanical inventions, best illustrated by the numerous devices described by Hero of Alexandria, whose treatise *Pneumatica* alone contains seventy-eight machines. Nearly all of these were designed for use in the temples to permit the priests to impress and awe the worshipers. Hero describes machines with siphons for producing such illusions as the conversion of water into wine. One contrivance enabled fires to be lit in hollow altars; the expansion of the air caused by the fire exerted pressures through concealed pipes, forcing libations of liquids onto the flame. In another device, the expanding air within the altar could be made to open the doors of the temple and later, when the fire cooled, to close them again. Hero is even credited with inventing the first coin-operated vending machine to dispense holy water.

That Hellenistic scientists like Hero, with their fertile inventive talents, did not apply their knowledge and imagination to industry is explained by the fact that the latter-day interaction between science and industry did not then exist. The scholarly intellectuals not only regarded the manual labor of the contemporary craftsman with disdain, but perhaps even more important, were little aware of how such craftsmen did their work.

In a word, the advance of technology faltered at the very moment when the intellectual ferment of the classical world seemed to imply great advances, because the organization of work delegated the industrial arts largely to slaves.

4. Ancient Agriculture: Family Farm and Slave Plantation

By far the greater part of the laboring population of the ancient world was engaged in agriculture. By far the greater part of the agricultural acreage, then as long after, was in family farms. Most ancient agriculture of all types—crop farming, stock raising, orchard farming—was small scale.

Even in those civilizations where the state owned the land, the allocation of farms was by family, and when large farming estates grew up, as in the Roman Empire, the structure of rural society was often scarcely affected because the rich landowner left the cultivation of the land to peasant clients, who farmed it in the traditional way.

Work within the family unit was divided on the basis of sex. Broadly speaking, the men of the farm bore the responsibility for the seasonal cycle of work and the women for the daily cycle. The farm family was an interdependent unit.

As with the city crafts, the method of learning agriculture techniques was an apprenticeship system, which had the effect of reinforcing and traditionalizing the sexual division of labor. The boys followed their father into the fields while the girls learned the household arts from their mother.

These domestic arts consisted primarily of food preparation and clothing manufacture and maintenance, both involving a number of laborious and exacting tasks. Before bread could be baked, the grain had to be ground in the quern, or hand mill, while before the clothing could be cut and sewn, the wool had to be spun and carded and the strands woven into cloth on the hand loom. Before soiled clothes could be washed, soap had to be made.

In the fields the usual draft team was a pair of yoked oxen, though it is possible that human traction was once used, and likely that where it was, the woman served as the plow animal. In ox plowing, two men or a man and a boy usually served as plowman and driver, the latter walking in front and guiding the animals.[1] The earlier agricultural civilizations used only wooden plows, unshod with iron. The iron plowshare was introduced in Greece by the time of Xenophon (fourth century B.C.).

In Greece the basic cereal crops were wheat and barley; in Rome, wheat, barley, and millet. In early times yields were very small, according to Hesiod (eighth century B.C.), about three to one, that is, a bushel of seed to produce three bushels of grain. By New Testament times yields had greatly improved, as suggested by the famous parable in Matthew in which the seed that fell "into good ground . . . brought forth fruit, some an hundredfold, some sixtyfold, some thirtyfold."[2] Pliny, writing at about the same time, optimistically asserts that the best soil gave a yield of 150 bushels of wheat to one of seed, but the usual Roman harvest was certainly far below that. Winter sowing was favored by the Romans to catch the main fall of moisture, but some spring sowing was done.[3]

With most crops there was a period of waiting after sowing, filled in partly by weeding and cultivating. Women often helped in these activities. At harvest time a tremendous collective effort was made, with all hands—men, women, and children—pressed into service to bring the mature crop in as rapidly as possible to cheat rain and frost. In Sumeria we know that the harvest gangs were broken into three-person teams, a reaper, a binder, and a sheaf-handler. The only harvest implement known was the iron sickle.

All hands also participated in winnowing—the separation of grain from chaff, usually by tossing it in the wind and catching the heavier grain while the light chaff blew away.

In winter, while the land lay fallow, the farmer occupied himself with carpentering in house and barn, repairing or making new harness and tools, patching roofs, and many other tasks. In a word, the organization of work on the small family farm of the ancient Mediterranean world presented a picture strikingly similar to that of the small family farm in most of the world in the nineteenth century, and much of it in the twentieth.

There were, however, larger farms or estates (latifundia) in which a more complex organization of work was in effect. Such treatises as those of Xenophon's *Oeconomicus* and Cato's *De Agricultura*[4] show an appreciation of the problems of rational farm management and an attempt to apply scientific principles. Most such works describe a farm of from sixty to seventy-five acres, in contrast to the small family farm of ten acres or less.

Xenophon is the first writer to stress the importance of the managerial function in large farming, advising the landlord to keep a sharp eye on his tenants in tilling, planting trees, sowing, and other activities. Cato recommends sowing fodder crops (beans, vetch, oats) in three successive plantings to produce a continuous supply, after which other crops were planted. Manure, precious and scanty because animals were few, should be carefully apportioned. Besides that of livestock, pigeon and other bird dung was saved, as was human waste. Vegetable fertilizers, including the dregs of olive oil, were used. On a medium estate devoted to olive orchards, Cato calculated that thirteen people were needed: an overseer, a housekeeper, five farm hands, three wool carders, one animal driver, one swineherd, and one shepherd. For the harvest, extra hands could be hired temporarily.

The great latifundia that developed under the Roman Empire, though appearing as early as the second century B.C., were usually characterized by absentee ownership because the owner was typically a man of great wealth who possessed several such huge estates. Direction of each was in the hands of a bailiff under whose command might be slaves numbering in the hundreds or even in a few cases in the thousands. Such slave labor was organized in gangs, each charged with different reponsibility.

One Roman landlord who d d in 8 B.C. left over 4,000 slaves, 7,200 oxen, and 257,000 other animals, mostly sheep and swine. Columella, who wrote in the first century

A.D. complains that on large latifundia most of the slaves mistreated the oxen and stole freely, but nevertheless thought that a capable and honest bailiff might make slave labor more profitable to the landlord than tenant farming.[5]

Besides free and slave farm labor there were the coloni, or serfs, either descendants of conquered cultivators of former times, bound to the land by their conquerors, or tenant farmers (sometimes former slaves) allotted lands for their own cultivation but legally bound to remain on it. These grew especially numerous in the later Roman Empire as the *Pax Romana* replaced the earlier aggressive wars and the source of supply of slaves dried up.

The size of the latifundia actually brought little improvement in the efficiency with which farming could be carried on. Given the primitive state of agricultural technology, a high ratio of men to area was unavoidable whether farms were small or large. However meager the farm worker's subsistence, he could produce little surplus beyond it, mainly because the limited number of animals so drastically limited the amount of fertilizer.

An element that did bring a certain amount of change in the agricultural picture was crop specialization.[6] In Greece and in Roman Italy the cultivation of cereal crops gradually became less profitable than specialized farming. In Greece, where the mountainous terrain was unfavorable to large-scale farming, the grape and the olive early became staple crops. At a later period the farmers of mainland Italy turned to vineyards and orchards while leaving cereal cultivation to the richer wheat lands of Sicily, North Africa, and Asia Minor. Crop specialization limited the self-sufficiency of farm units and brought a demand for specialists, for example, to produce containers for storage and transport of wine and olive oil, both of which were shipped long distance by land and sea. Wheat itself became a specialized crop and was imported to imperial Rome from Egypt and elsewhere in large volume. A sizable shipping industry was created, with many other specialist occupations.

Livestock farming was of course also practiced in the ancient world. Typically the goats and sheep in Greece and the Near East were driven up in the hills in summer and back to the valleys in winter (transhumance). Cattle and horses were grazed only in the lowlands. Probably the work was given over principally to boys and older men, though we have no evidence of the division of labor. Apparently no attempt at selective breeding was made; even in early Roman times the animals were allowed to graze freely and mate randomly. But by the first century A.D., Varro, Columella, and Vergil all emphasized the importance of selective breeding, at least for sheep. Valued principally for its wool but also for its milk, the sheep was given great attention, one shepherd being assigned to each hundred rough-wooled sheep and one to each fifty fine-wooled animals. Goats were also selectively bred, especially for milk, and pigs for meat.

In summary, it may be said that the organization of work and agricultural technology were little advanced over Neolithic times, and that the basic condition of the farmer remained the same: tiny acreage, few and crude implements, few crops, low yields, high hazard. At best he scraped a difficult living from the soil, and at worst, which came all too often, he and his family were suddenly confronted, through the vagaries of drought, storm, pests, disease, war, or other calamity, with the threat of famine. Yet some significant improvements appeared in Roman agriculture, even though they were little exploited in Roman times. In addition to specialized farming, the three-field system, with fodder crops to provide subsistence for animals, was introduced in some regions of Italy. The waterwheel was applied to the grinding of grain, though not widely. A wheeled plow was invented, though scarcely used. All these awaited the Middle Ages for intensive application.

One other Roman development is worthy of extended notice—the growth of specialized crafts, both in the country and in the town.

5. Ancient Industry:
Craftsmen and the
Hand Factory

Besides the influence of specialized agriculture, the growth of urban crafts was fostered by the development of larger markets and more sophisticated tastes. Despite the economic difficulties that increasingly racked the Roman Empire in its later stages, a wealthy class survived and supplied a market for many kinds of craft goods. Even mass production of a sort was encouraged, with large workshops devoted to craft production of a single product.[1]

Specialized craftsmen were of course nothing new in Roman times. The earliest were probably itinerant, moving from place to place to provide more or less regular services as smiths, leather workers, shield makers, and other specialists. As the market grew and demand increased, these craftsmen no longer found it necessary to quit their homes, which became their shops. Their products traveled rather than the workmen themselves.

In the code of Hammurabi (eleventh century B.C.) and in the Homeric epics (900-800 B.C.), mention is made of only a few specialized crafts designed to produce for the local city-state market: carpenter, blacksmith, potter, shipbuilder, housebuilder, armorer. As Mediterranean commerce grew, especially in the Hellenistic period (after 323 B.C.) and the specialties of one region were traded for those of another, important changes developed in production. Certain cities specialized in certain commodities, *e.g.*, Athens in pottery, and Pompeii in wool finishing. The distinction between production for a smaller unit and that for a larger economic entity can be seen in a famous passage from Xenophon's *Cyropaedia* (fourth century B.C.) describing craft production in the Persian Empire.

> In small towns the same workman makes chairs and doors and plows and tables, and often the same artisan builds houses. . . . And it is, of course, impossible for a man of many trades to be proficient in all of them. In large cities, on the other hand, inasmuch as many people have demands to make upon each branch of industry, one trade alone, and very often even less than a whole trade, is enough to support a man: one man, for instance, makes shoes for men, and another for women; and there are places even where one man earns a living by only stitching shoes, another by cutting them out, another by sewing the uppers together, while there is another who performs none of these operations but only assembles the parts.[2]

Specialization extended to household tasks. Xenophon's *Oeconomicus* describes the preparations of food in a large household: "Each has his special task, one boiling the meat, another roasting it, one doing the fish in spiced sauce, another frying it, and another making the bread. . . ."

Similarly, in pottery making, the shaping, firing, and decoration were sometimes carried out in different establishments.[3] Not all pottery establishments made the same kind of ware. Distinctions grew up among those which made cooking pots, jars, goblets, and funerary urns. In woodworking, similar distinctions developed among makers of couches, chests, and caskets.[4] Pliny even cites a case of a geographical division between elements of the same industry: candelabra whose bases were made in Tarentum and whose upper parts were manufactured in Aegina.

As the number of crafts and the number of craftsmen in each multiplied, the practitioners of the various skills tended to collect in certain quarters of the city or on certain streets for the convenience of customers and suppliers. This congregation of specialists led to one of the most far-reaching and long-lasting socioeconomic innovations of the ancient world: the craft corporation or guild.[5] In its beginnings the craft association was evidently religious-social in character. Each association had its patron god or goddess, and its members held their own communal religious services, while a mutual-aid function similar to that of modern trade unions included funds for sickness and burial. But in time the guilds came to undertake the regulation of production and fixing of standards. In the Roman Empire the government gave its sanction and reinforcement to the guild movement, out of an interest in assuring continuity of craft production and in regulating it for the benefit of the state. Ultimately the Roman corporations became so closely controlled that they functioned virtually as a part of the state apparatus.

Related to the historical development of craft guilds was the tendency toward occupational heredity, a trend best documented, like the guild movement, in Rome. The naturalness of occupational heredity—a father teaching his son his trade—is evident enough, but in the later Roman Empire it received the powerful sanction of law. The reason lay in the general economic decay that affected various occupations unevenly, rendering some ill-paid or debt-ridden. Practitioners of these crafts naturally sought to escape into more lucrative or easier work. Consequently, among the "reforms" of Diocletian (reigned A.D. 284-305) were laws compelling sons to follow in their fathers' footsteps lest trades essential to the state wither. Among these essential occupations were those of the millers and bakers who supplied Rome with bread, the carpenters and masons who built and maintained the public buildings, the armorers and ironworkers who equipped the legions, and the transport workers on land and sea. Eventually, as the catastrophic economic decline of Rome continued, the reactionary and harmful system was extended to nearly all crafts and professions. There is little doubt that Diocletian's laws received support from popular attitudes, which favored people's staying in "their place" and frowned on upward mobility.

Specialization in certain crafts led to an increase in the scale of shop production. Pottery, long the art of a single craftsman working alone, spawned shops of from twelve to fifteen men, working under a master who organized his subordinates in the interests of efficiency and economy. Some mixed clay, some shaped urns and handles (for the largest containers, the amphoras used for long-distance commerce in wine and oil, two men operated the potter's wheel), some painted (with assistants to help prepare colors and varnishes), some glazed, and some fired. Yet the scale of production did not increase beyond the shop with a dozen assistants, because all ceramic wares could be made with simple equipment and there was nothing to be gained from a larger concentration of workers. Even in cases where a single master owned several workshops, all operated independently. The largest pottery shops known in records of the ancient world employed as many as seventy men, but these were very rare, and amounted essentially to a mere amalgam of several smaller shops.[6]

Perhaps the most important craft practiced both domestically and for commercial production was cloth-making. Techniques for both kinds of production were identical.[7] The chief textiles of the ancient world were wool, cotton, and linen. All three required spinning the fiber into thread and weaving the thread on a loom. Cotton fibers in the Near East were very short, and as the fibers were drawn out from the bundle held by the distaff, they were twisted on a spindle resting in a bowl or on the ground to steady it against an accidental jerk that might break the fragile thread. Wool fibers had two advantages over cotton; they were longer and had a scaly quality that made them catch on or mesh with other fibers, making the spun thread stronger and more resilient than cotton. Wool spinners did not need to rest their spindles on the ground, and if they stood instead of sitting a longer thread could be spun before it was wound on the spindle. Wool spinners also found that the rhythm of walking helped the spinning, and often spun as they moved their flocks during transhumance migrations, a practice that helped diffuse the art of spinning.

Linen could be spun in the same way, but the fibers were

moistened during spinning because it was found that the drying action strengthened the thread. But an entirely different technique was also used with linen, as is shown in a model of a weaving shop from an Egyptian tomb of about 2000 B.C. Here women are shown sitting along the wall of the shop with heaps of flax in front of them. Two small bundles of flax were taken at a time, the ends lapped about two inches and the splice rolled against the right thigh. The action was repeated to splice on another little bundle, making a roving. The rovings were put into a jug of water, from which they were presently taken and joined to form a length of yarn. This kind of Egyptian linen may be what the writer of Exodus 26:1 meant: "Moreover thou shalt make the tabernacle with ten curtains of fine twined linen, and blue, and purple, and scarlet: with cherubims of cunning work shalt thou make them."

This would be in contrast to the more familiar method indicated by Exodus 35:25. "And all the women that were wise hearted did spin with their hands, and brought that which they had spun, both of blue, and of purple, and of scarlet, and of fine linen."

Looms were likewise adapted to the type of fiber being woven. For linen cloth the early Egyptians used a wide horizontal loom operated by two women, but about 1450 B.C. stood it upright by adding a post on either side, an arrangement that allowed gravity to assist in pushing the weft threads in and out of the standing warp threads.

The Greek loom, renowned in antiquity, was designed primarily for weaving wool.[8] It was a vertical loom, with the warp ends widely spaced at the bottom, in front of which the weaver stood to lace the wefts in and out. This arrangement made it easy for the weaver to put in a new yarn, and consequently the Greeks were the first to weave color patterns.

A third type of loom was developed in India for weaving cotton. It was horizontal, like the early Egyptian loom, but with a special feature: the odd warp yarns were threaded on one harness and the even on another that could be raised and lowered by a foot pedal, leaving both the weaver's hands free to maneuver the fragile cotton weft.

The spinning and weaving operations remained essentially unchanged throughout the long period of classical antiquity, but considerable improvements were made in finishing operations. Sophisticated equipment was developed for fulling and dyeing, and operated by a specialized labor force, usually made up of women, and sometimes entirely slave, including the foreman.

Fulling, which included both the cleaning of cloth and the beating of it to coalesce the yarns into a solid texture, was nearly always divorced from domestic spinning and weaving, probably because it required an extensive system of vats, water supply, and chemicals—the absorbent clay known as fuller's earth, animal urine, and mineral alkali. Other finishing processes on wool cloth, such as napping, or brushing to make the nap thicken, required special tools and skill. Wool was washed twice, the raw fleece receiving a thorough scouring to remove dirt, suint (sweat), and lanolin. The fleece was first soaked in warm water to dissolve impurities, with the herb soapwort used as a cleansing agent. After washing, the fleece was beaten with sticks to knock out the dirt. The delicacy of wool fiber, which can be damaged by too hot water or too strong a detergent, dictated that the wool-scourer also be a skilled craftsman.

Dyeing even more than fulling required high skill and

complicated equipment, and for this reason certain cities became centers of finished cloth production, often specializing in a particular kind of dye. Tarentum, Puteoli, and Ancona in Italy specialized in the purple dye famous throughout the Roman Empire. Syracuse, Cumae, and Canusium were known for the fineness of their wools, while Parma and Modena in the north produced coarser wools for everyday wear. Padua specialized in linen, as did Etruria, while Rome was noted for the quality of its embroidery.

Pompeii, the first-century A.D. storehouse of so much of our knowledge of the social life of the Roman world, had a vigorous wool industry, with many fulleries, dyehouses, and scouring shops, and a combination of wool exchange and fullers' guildhall (the *Eumachia*). Pompeii's skilled dyers specialized in particular colors, and each was known by the name of his specialty: the cerinarius did yellow dyeing; the violarius, violet; the flammarius, red; the crocotarius, saffron; the spadicarius, brown; the purpurarius, purple; and the atramentarius, black. This division was doubtless occasioned by the technical problems presented by the wool fibers and the different kinds of dyes, and is a clear indication of the degree of craft specialization in the Roman Empire.[9]

The arms industry was another in which there was both a high degree of specialization and relatively large-scale shop production. Some armorers specialized in helmets, others in swords, pikes, or shields. Because of a dependably high demand, production did not have to be in response to orders, but could be used for stockpiling. An Athenian workshop of the fifth century B.C. employed 32 slaves to produce knives, while a shield factory at Lysias employed 120.[10] Yet there was little standardization of military equipment, a proof of the fact that production was carried on in modest workshops directed by individual masters like those of the pottery industry.

The chief examples of large-scale production in the ancient world are provided by mining and metallurgy. The geographical concentration and isolation of the mines and the nature of the work made the employment of fairly large work crews necessary. The severe working conditions of the mines dictated that the labor be carried on mainly by slaves. Free men were loath to enter the Greek and Roman mines, which were exploited under compulsion and force. In the silver mines at Laurium, one of the foundations of the commercial glory of Athens, men worked ten-hour shifts, followed by ten hours of rest, in dark and narrow passages lighted by smoking lanterns that made the air nearly unbreathable. Three work gangs toiled under command of a master miner. Five men, of sturdy strength, swung pickaxes at the ore face. Some twenty weaker men or young boys carried the material out of the mine, and outside the working, a third gang of women and old men sifted the ore from the rock.[11]

Metallurgy was carried on in close conjunction with mining. A master smelter supervised workmen divided into three groups: crushers of the ore—the strongest worked the mortar, the weakest the hand mill—the washers, and the smelters. Because furnaces and hand bellows were small, smelting was necessarily done in small batches. Metal was not, of course, a basic industrial material in the sense of a later age. Gold and silver were used for ornamentation and in coinage, and copper, tin, zinc, and iron, for weapons and tools. Once the metal was separated from the ore, many specialized crafts were called into operation: pattern-makers, turners, metal-chasers, gilders, goldsmiths and silversmiths. Bronze workers, using alloys of copper and tin or copper and zinc (the modern distinction between bronze and brass is blurred in ancient and Biblical references), made pots, jugs, chafing dishes, tripods, and decorated tableware as well as weapons and tools. Such creations were more the product of an artisan than an industrial worker, and often more the product of an artist than an artisan.

The Roman Empire saw the craftsman emerge as a producer for a general market who no longer had to wait for a specific order to make a custom product. Craft work, however, not only continued to be based on specialized skills, but the skills became even more highly specialized. Yet this specialization was not forced, as we shall see was the case in a later period, by the demands of machines. The workman continued to control his own working action. He modified the form of his product according to his own skill, taste, and judgment, the results of which were visible to him in the finished job. Even where a craftsman did not himself make the entire product, as in the case of the wool dyers, he could clearly see the effect of his own handiwork.

Thus despite the undoubted hardships of his life, the Roman craft worker enjoyed a large sphere of independent action in his work, and from it probably derived a considerable satisfaction.

6. Ancient Engineering: Large-Scale Construction by Conscript Labor

Truly large-scale organization of labor was never achieved in ancient societies in the production of commodities. Yet many ancient societies exhibited a capacity to mobilize labor on a large scale that has astonished the world ever since. In the construction of the monumental public works of Egypt, Greece, Rome, India, China, and other ancient civilizations, the engineers were handicapped by a triple lack: the lack of powered machinery, the lack of sophisticated mechanical devices, and the lack of suitable harnesses to make the most of animal power.

Equipped with neither wheeled transport nor pulleys, Egyptian engineers were confronted with an apparently insuperable task in moving blocks of granite weighing two and a half tons to the site of the Pyramids and raising them into place. Yet they made good their deficiency in machinery for materials-handling by a superb organization of human labor.[1] The Great Pyramid of Khufu (Cheops) at Gizeh, built about 2500 B.C., is composed of 2,300,000 enormous blocks of granite, diorite, limestone, and basalt. To quarry so vast a quantity of stone, dress it, transport it to the site, and place it, in a space of time believed to be only twenty years, would be a nearly incredible feat even with the aid of wheel and pulley. Without them, the construction involved a highly rationalized organization of a labor force believed to have numbered 30,000 throughout the project. The mere logistics of housing and feeding such an army would severely tax a technologically weak society. Most of the workers were free peasants, conscripted to work on the Pyramid as a form of labor tax during the season of the Nile flooding when they could not toil in the fields. They were not regarded as expendable; on the contrary, the overseers and foremen took pride in reporting on the safety and welfare of their men. Among the fragmentary records is one in which the leader of an expedition to a desert quarry boasted that he had not lost a man or a mule.

The master builder of each of the Pyramids was a trusted noble of the court and advisor of the Pharaoh. Some of them are known to us by name, of whom the most famous is Imhotep, high priest to the Pharaoh Zoser and architect of the world's oldest surviving man-made structure, Zoser's step-pyramid at Saqqarah of about 2680 B.C. Most of the pyramid builders were doubtless, like Imhotep, public officials with a broad range of talents and responsibilities. Imhotep was renowned as a sage and his sayings immortalized in the Wisdom Books of Egypt. Some twenty-three centuries after his death he was deified as the god of medicine, the Greeks equating him with their own god of healing,

Aesculapius, and his tomb became a shrine for pilgrims seeking cures.

Under the master builder labored a large hierarchy of subordinates, superintendents, and foremen, each with his scribes and recorders. The various labor gangs who worked on the Pyramids were imbued with a spirit of pride in their work, as is shown by the fact that they inscribed their team names in red ocher on the great stones they cut. Blocks of the Meidum Pyramid bear such names as "Steppe Pyramid Gang," "Boat Gang," "Vigorous Gang," "Sceptre Gang," and "Enduring Gang." The names may also have facilitated keeping track of the amount of stone quarried by each gang.[2]

Granite for the columns, architraves, door jambs, lintels, and casing blocks was quarried at Aswan, up the Nile from the pyramid site. The quarrying involved many specialized tasks. Stone boulders were cut out of the rock by drilling a line of holes along the grain, inserting wedges of sycamore or acacia in the holes, and soaking the wedges with water until they swelled enough to crack the stone neatly along the grain. If no grain could be found, the wooden wedges were inserted and set fire, and, at their hottest, doused with cold water to crack the rock.

The stones were cut into shape by bronze saws set with jewels, either corundum or diamond. Where hollows were required they were made by tubular drilling, utilizing the same principles as modern diamond rock drills, with one man turning the drill while the other supplied the percussion with a hammer.

It was long believed that the Egyptians moved their huge stone blocks on rollers, but modern research has discovered that their technique was to lay greased boards under the blocks and slide them forward.[3]

Specialized craftsmen were doubtless numerous at the construction site—carpenters, for example, were needed to dismantle ramps and falsework—but unfortunately we know almost nothing of the details of this most impressive of the works of antiquity. One of the tantalizing mysteries of the Pyramids is the fact that when one was finished and ready to serve as the mausoleum of a reigning Pharaoh, another was often begun immediately. It has been suggested that the huge monuments had a character as public-works projects to insure full employment during the Nile flood periods.

The Egyptians are also known to have dug a Suez canal. Some ancient accounts claim that the Pharaoh Sesostris constructed a canal from a tributary on the Nile Delta to the Gulf of Suez in about 2000 B.C. Herodotus states that the Pharaoh Necho, about 700 B.C., built a canal across the isthmus connecting the Mediterranean and Red Seas, "four days' journey in length, and wide enough for two armies abreast." This canal may have been completed some time later, under the Ptolemies, who are known to have several times restored it. Despite this, the canal was not navigable in the late first century B.C., when Cleopatra attempted to use it to flee after the battle of Actium. The canal was later twice restored, once by the emperor Trajan (98-117) and again by the Arab invaders of the seventh century A.D., but each time it soon filled in and fell into disuse.

We know considerably more of the much later monumental works of the Greeks and Romans. In many cases we know the names of the builders, for example, the architects Callicrates and Ictinus who were responsible for the Parthenon. Under them worked master masons, sculptors, carpenters, and smiths, each at the head of a team of laborers. The masters were generally free citizens or metics (free foreigners living in Athens), while most of the laborers were slaves. That the work was organized efficiently is evident from the customary form of contract, by which the Athenian government specified the character of the work and laid down a time limit in which it was to be completed. Specialization of labor was increasingly marked on the Greek public works; in building the temple at Delos in the Hellenistic period, a joiner who fitted a door did not set up the post to hold it, and the stone masons did not sharpen their own tools, but had assistants to perform the task. Rules governing Hellenistic craft specialties resembled those of modern building trades.

The greatest public works builders of the ancient world were of course the Romans.[4] They were almost alone in constructing massive works of a purely secular character: roads, bridges, tunnels, aqueducts, baths, amphitheaters, harbors, and lighthouses. While Roman engineers enjoyed many technical advantages over their Egyptian predecessors—the wheel, the pulley, the arch, the vault, a good natural mortar—they were nevertheless seriously handicapped in their lack of scientific knowledge, especially of the strength of materials and forms. They knew only the semicircular arch and for vaulting relied almost exclusively on the barrel vault derived from it. In consequence they built enormously massive structures whose great weight was often a drawback in the finished work and always created difficult problems during construction. Despite this, Roman engineers confidently took on such stupendous tasks as the Pont du Gard in Gaul and the Segovian Aqueduct in Spain, fitting the huge stone jigsaw puzzles together so meticulously that they required no mortar to stand for the next twenty centuries. The expert organization of men and materials was the key to such successes. In

Rome, especially under the Republic, a steady supply of slaves, many of them skilled workers, was furnished by the wars of conquest.

Roman systematization and discipline are especially noteworthy in bridgebuilding. Stone-arch bridges were rarely built before the Romans, but by the first century A.D. the Romans were adept at their construction. The oldest surviving bridge in the city of Rome, the Pons Milvius, dates from 109 B.C. The Roman method was to build a cofferdam in the river by driving a wide double circle of piles, and filling the intervening space with clay. The interior of the cofferdam was dewatered and kept dry, or at least shallow, by one gang of slaves while another dug away at the river bottom. When they struck bedrock, or were in water up to their necks, the piles were driven—alder, olive, or oak saplings, charred and driven in by a weight lifted by a capstan wheel. When the piles were driven as deep as they could be made to go (to "refusal") they were sawed off evenly, the interstices filled with stone and mortar, and the rock-and-rubble pier foundations constructed on top. Very little improvement on the Roman technique was made in the succeeding millennium and a half.

The Roman engineers' organizational talent may also be seen in their town planning. New cities were built in Gaul and other provinces with streets laid out in strict geometric pattern, with public buildings, baths, theaters, fountains, and monuments sited for convenience and beauty, and with regulations formulated for height of private buildings and for traffic flow. Water supply and sewage disposal were provided. In the all-encompassing character of their planning, involving careful weighing of economic factors, calculation of engineering costs, allowance for military, commercial, political, and religious requirements, and in the successful coordination of several engineering disciplines, the Roman engineers and town planners foreshadowed much of the approach employed by modern systems engineering.

7. Disintegration and Recovery: Medieval Technology

The later stages of the western Roman Empire coincided with the phenomenon known to history as the "great migrations," the long-distance movements of peoples that affected large parts of Europe and Asia and that apparently had their origin in still unexplained cataclysms in Central Asia. What is clear is that a domino effect developed, with Asian nomads pouring into eastern and central Europe displacing native peoples who moved west and south, entering the Roman Empire sometimes as peaceful immigrants, sometimes as invading hosts. The economically troubled western Empire, unable either to halt or to absorb such vast incursions, disintegrated politically into a number of fragments, with widespread social and economic chaos.

The dislocation of long-distance commerce brought on a powerful tendency toward the small, self-sufficient economic unit, which heightened the political fragmentation. Completing the vicious circle, the breakup of western Europe into tiny political principalities made the restoration of commerce difficult. The Dark Ages, thus inaugurated and sustained, lasted from the fifth to the tenth century. The disappearance of large-scale demand meant the radical reduction in scale of production, and the substitution of the small, self-sustaining feudal economic units put a premium on the jack-of-all-trades in contrast to the specialized craftsman of more prosperous times. The manorial community, a cluster of a few dozen or a few score people almost entirely supporting themselves, did not require an expert harness-maker, a wheelwright, a carpenter; it needed a man who could perform passably at all three tasks and many others besides. A few specialists survived and even flourished—the armorer, for one. Some regional specialization also survived, such as textile manufacture in the Low Countries, and long-distance trade never ceased entirely. At the depth of the Dark Ages Jewish traders called Radanites carried on a remarkable, if small-scale commerce between western Europe and the Far East, journeying by sea from France to Egypt, and thence overland to Persia, India, and China.[1] Yet the Europe-wide economic slowdown precipitated by the migrations continued, aggravated first by the Moslem raiders of the seventh and eighth centuries and then by the Viking pirates of the ninth.

It would be a mistake, however, to regard the Dark Ages as a total loss either socially, economically, or technologically. Slavery, the outright ownership of human beings as chattels, declined rapidly under the combined pressures of the spread of Christian doctrine, the disintegration of the Roman Empire, and the disappearance of both the great slave plantations and the slave-built monumental works. A slave trade persisted, with the Slavs of the Balkan peninsula, who gave their name to the European word, supplying most of the material, the Italians, especially the Venetians, most actively engaged, and the Arabs supplying the market, but this too gradually declined. French medievalist Marc Bloch advanced the thesis that the revulsion of the Christian life outlook against slavery (even in the Middle Ages to enslave a Christian was regarded as criminal) gradually caused a tightening of the labor market that stimulated the search for labor-saving technology.[2]

Christianity was responsible for another philosophical contribution of far-reaching significance. In place of the intellectual disdain for manual labor of classical antiquity, the monastic order of the Benedictines substituted a sturdy defense of the value of honest toil under the slogan *Laborare est orare* (To work is to pray). Benedictine Rule XLVIII specified, "Idleness is the enemy of the soul and therefore, at fixed times, the brothers ought to be occupied in manual labor, and again at fixed times, in sacred reading."[3] This breaching of the old barrier between intellectual contemplation and work created a new atmosphere congenial to the marriage of theory and practice.

Significantly the monks encouraged the development of labor-saving devices—work was good, not simply for its own sake, but for the results it achieved. Actively and by example, the Benedictines, Cistercians, Cluniacs, and other great monastic orders contributed to the felling of the forests and clearing of the land that made room for a vast expansion of agriculture in western Europe.

Important technical innovations also marked the Dark Ages, either as new inventions or as importations from the East. The migrant people introduced the stirrup, which the Frankish chief Charles Martel combined with the high-pommeled saddle to create the armored knight. This new kind of warrior had an enormous social and economic impact, becoming the principal building block of the new feudal system. In central Europe in the sixth century appeared a new model of plow, much heavier than the traditional Roman plow, and mounted on wheels. Armed with a separate vertical blade (coulter) to dig under the soil and a mouldboard to turn it over, this new plow made possible the exploitation for agriculture of the rich bottom lands of northwest Europe. Because its weight required cooperative effort, including the pooling of oxen, it contributed to the communal pattern of the feudal-manorial system. Controversy persists over a puzzling feature of medieval plowing with oxen; repeated references in manorial documents to teams of eight oxen remain mystifying. Such large traction power was not needed for plowing, and not a single example of an eight-ox team appears in the extensive pictorial evidence, *i.e.*, the Bayeux tapestry and the Luttrell Psalter, which show only two-oxen and (occasionally) four-oxen teams. One theory is that eight oxen were necessary for plowing up newly cleared forest land; another is that the eight-ox team is an economic rather than technical unit.[4] In any case, a single farmer could not manage even a pair of oxen alone. As in ancient times, a driver was required to guide the team while the plowman manned the plow. Sometimes, according to an English manuscript, the plowman "holdeth the plough stilt [handle] in his left hand, and in his right the plough staff to break the clods." More commonly the plow team was followed up by women and children armed with sticks to break the clods.

Not only did the new plow succeed in tilling the heavy soil of western Europe that the old Roman scratch plow could not cultivate, but it turned the soil over so thoroughly that the Roman system of cross-plowing—going over a field twice, the second time at right angles to the first—could be eliminated, a valuable economy of time and labor.

A major innovation that appeared in Europe in the ninth century was the rigid, padded horse collar, probably an importation from the East. The horse collar made it possible for the first time effectively to employ horses for traction. Later in the same century the nailed horseshoe solved the problem of the crippling wear of horses' hooves.

The combination of the horse and the wheeled plow was related to another agricultural innovation: the three-field system. Since time immemorial, farmers had plowed one half of their land every year, alternating the halves to permit the soil to recover its fertility. The introduction of legume cultivation helped make possible a more efficient three-field system, in which one-third of an arable piece of land was left fallow all year, one-third planted to traditional cereal crops in the autumn, and one-third to oats, barley, and legumes in the spring, to be harvested in late summer. The legumes (beans and peas) strengthened the soil through their nitrogen-fixing ability, so that the land could remain fertile despite the more intensive cultivation. The oats provided fodder for the new horse population, while the beans and peas improved the diet of the human population.[5]

The Romans had experimented with a three-field system in some regions of Italy, but it was not till the Middle Ages that the new technological developments made possible its wide application. The change from two-field to three-field system increased agricultural production by one-third to one-half, providing the surpluses needed to support a non-farming population.

The new combination of stock-raising with crop production, two agricultural pursuits that had been kept separated in the ancient world, helped foster the characteristic communal organization of the Middle Ages called the "open field system." This system prevailed in the area of "champion" country, comprising most of the plain of northern Europe and a band of England from the North Sea Coast through the Midlands to the Channel. Champion country was characterized by large villages and open stretches of arable land, contrasting with the "woodland" country of Normandy and Brittany and of western and southeastern England, where small individual farms enclosed with hedges and ditches were the rule and tiny hamlets replaced the villages.[6]

Communal organization in champion country was made imperative by the system of land tenure, the division of arable land within the village community, and the method of plowing. Half or more of the arable land was "held" by the peasant cultivators, though not owned outright, while the rest belonged to the lord. The peasants worked on the lord's land (the demesne) for a certain number of days each week throughout the year, plowing, reaping, moving, shocking, and transporting grain, threshing and winnowing, washing and shearing sheep. Some of the villagers, usually boys and old men, were detailed for herding duty. The arable land was divided into large fields, two or three depending on whether the two- or three-field system prevailed, which were then subdivided into long narrow strips. The strips also reflected the efficacy of the new heavy plow, with its elimination of cross-plowing. Each peasant held several strips in each field, and the lord's demesne land was likewise scattered in strips among the fields. The purpose of this arrangement was to ensure equity in good and bad soils and locations. Because of it, and because of the need to pool oxen for plow teams, farm work was probably at least partly communal, though there is evidence that there was private plowing and reaping. A dishonest peasant in *Piers Plowman* confesses: "If I went to the plow I pinched so narrowly that I would steal a foot of land or a furrow, or gnaw the half-acre of my neighbor; and if I reaped, I would over-reap [reach over into his neighbor's ground], or gave counsel to those that reaped to seize for me with their sickles that which I never sowed."[7] A thirteenth-century moralistic work translated into English by Robert Mannyng of Brunne as *Handlyng Synne* condemns "false husbandmen who falsely plow away men's lands."[8] On the lord's lands, peasants worked as a body, but on their own lands cooperation may have been local and sporadic.

A feature of the services which the peasants performed for the lords was the movable works, called *precarie*, boons, or benes, due during the crises of the farming year, when plowing, moving, or reaping had to be done in a hurry to take advantage of good weather. All the villagers worked for the lord at these times, in return for food or drink or money, or all three. Like the barn-raisings and bees of a later era, these workdays were social occasions, and sometimes ended in a "sporting chance," when the lord gave each of the hay-makers as much hay as he could lift with his scythe, or gave the reapers a sheep to roast if they could catch it.

The later Middle Ages multiplied communal village regulations. Typical of the "bylaws" enacted by English villagers to govern work in the critical harvest period is a code from Halton, Buckinghamshire, of 1329:

> It is ordained by the lord's bailiffs and by the community of the whole homage, as well the freemen as the villeins [serfs], that no one shall glean who can get for a

day's work a penny and his food. Also, that the gleaners shall glean as well and faithfully as their youth or age will allow. Also, that no one shall take in outsiders or natives who behave themselves badly in the gleaning or elsewhere. . . . Also, that no one may go into the fields with a cart after sunset to carry corn. Also, that no one may enter onto the stubbles with sheep or other beasts before they have been depastured by the beasts of the plow. . . . Also that no one hereafter may gather in the fields beans or green peas save between half of prime and prime.[9]

Thus no able-bodied man, capable of reaping, was permitted to do the much lighter work of gleaning, that is, following up the reapers to pick what they had missed, a task reserved for the women and the very young and very old. Other bylaws prescribed that gleaning should not begin until the sheaves were in, or that gleaners should remain a furlong behind reapers. Everything should be done in the daytime when no thieving was possible.

The open field system allowed scant room for individual initiative. Everyone had to follow rigid rules laid down by custom, and the clever or skilled farmer had little advantage over the incompetent.

Revolutionary changes also took place in transport. Refinements in harness, especially the addition of the whipple-tree, facilitating turning, made the rapid-gaited horse the premier animal for transport.

An equally far-reaching technical development affected water transport. The triangular fore-and-aft ("lateen" for Latin) sail, which could be manipulated to catch the wind on either quarter, making tacking possible, became important in the Mediterranean as early as the sixth century, although it had not been unknown to classical sailors.[10] The magnetic compass and the sternpost rudder of the high Middle Ages completed the maritime revolution, but even in the earlier period the new sail immensely facilitated sea commerce.

An important innovation of about the year 1000 was the application of the waterwheel to purposes other than the grinding of grain. Three types of vertical waterwheel were used in medieval Europe: undershot, breast, and overshot, the designations referring to the point at which the current of water hit the wheel's revolving paddles or buckets. Most medieval waterwheels were motivated by streams, either natural or man-built (millraces), but in certain places on the seacoast tidal flow was exploited. Horizontal wheels were also used extensively, but only for grinding grain.

The new technology[11] combined with certain economic trends to foster a general revival, discernible by the early eleventh century, and greatly stimulated by the Crusades, which gave Italian commercial cities valuable bases in the East. The agricultural revolution that had by now turned western European forests into productive farmland was supplemented by a "Commercial Revolution," as modern medieval scholars have called it, centering in Italy and Flanders, that built new cities and expanded old ones. The old crafts and industries began to revive, and were soon supplemented by new. The fragmentation into small feudal estates was reversed, bringing larger political agglomerations and eventually national monarchies. Stability and expansion restored interdependence between town and countryside and among regions. Conditions were once more established for the continued development of the division of labor and the organization of work.

8. Medieval Work: Guilds and the Putting-Out System

One of the most striking phenomena of the high Middle Ages is the reappearance, in an even more vigorous form, of the ancient craft guilds. The origin of the medieval guilds is something of a scholarly puzzle, though apparently in Italy, the most economically advanced region of Europe, some guilds had a continuous existence from Roman times. In any case, the proliferation of crafts and craftsmen in northwest Europe in the eleventh and twelfth centuries was accompanied by the revival or foundation of scores of guilds whose masters were a combination of merchant-craftsmen selling the products of their shop at their front door. Among early records are those of weavers' guilds in Mainz by 1099, fishmongers in Worms by 1106, shoemakers at Würzburg in 1128, and craft guilds of various types in London, Lincoln, Oxford, and other English towns in the reign of Henry I (1100-1135). The basic explanation for the medieval craft guilds is simply that the Middle Ages were the supreme period of craft skill.

Many of the new guilds were entirely unknown to the ancient world. The carpenter, originally both a housebuilder and furniture maker, divided into carpenter and joiner, the latter using lighter and more precise tools to fashion cabinets and other interior woodwork. A third craft, that of the wood-carver, split off for the most delicate work. Eventually the painting of the finished wood products devolved upon still another new craft.

By the thirteenth century there were well over a hundred guilds in Paris, the largest city in northwest Europe. Among the most important were shoemakers, furriers, tailors, barbers, jewelers, cooks, bakers, masons, carpenters, weavers, chandlers, mercers, coopers, scabbard makers, hatmakers, saddlers, purse makers, porters, butchers, fishmongers, plasterers, blacksmiths, painters, roofers, locksmiths, ropemakers, tanners, copyists, sculptors, rug makers, cutlers, glovemakers, and wood carvers.[1] Not surprisingly, by the fourteenth-century disputes were arising as guilds impinged on their neighbors. Like their Roman predecessors, medieval guilds provided welfare assistance to their members, but their chief function was to protect the craft as a whole by strict regulation of production. The aim of a great mass of guild legislation in respect to quality control was to prevent unfair competition and to protect the guild's market.

The officers of a guild took an oath on the relics of a saint to "guard the guild" carefully and loyally, and to spare neither friends nor relatives caught foisting substandard goods on the consuming public. Precise quantities and types of raw materials were specified. Ale could have no constituents save grain, hops, and water. Chandlers had to use four pounds of tallow for each quarter pound of wick. Makers of bone handles were forbidden by their guild to trim their products with silver lest they pass them off for ivory. The guild of clothes menders forbade its members to press, fold, and hang garments, lest they be tempted to fob off their secondhand merchandise as new. Inspection visits were made by guild officers, scales checked, substandard goods confiscated. A jeweler found using colored glass instead of stones paid a heavy fine.

In the interest of preserving fair competition, work on Sundays and saints' days was banned, thus preventing the impious from gaining an unfair advantage over the pious. Night work was forbidden both in the interest of fair competition and because poor light compromised meticulous workmanship; work hours, fixed from dawn to dusk, were long in summer and shorter in winter. The salesman side of the guild member's profession was also regulated. The craftsman-merchant was forbidden to solicit customers by hawking his merchandise in the streets or from door to door (with certain exceptions, such as the fishmongers). At St. Omer in Flanders regulations forbade greeting a passerby from one's shop, or even blowing one's nose or sneezing to attract attention. Boatmen bringing beer to Bruges were forbidden to display notices advertising their product. The guilds also sought, with varying success, to fix prices and wages.

Most guilds were divided simply into masters and apprentices, but in some by the thirteenth century a middle grade, valet or journeyman, was introduced. Masters were generally allowed only one or two apprentices (brewers, shoemakers, grocers, and a few others were permitted more), but all masters could employ as many sons, brothers, or nephews as they wished, a reflection of the ancient hereditary character of the crafts. The apprentice started out with the most menial tasks, acting as sweeper, cleaner, porter, shop and errand boy, and often as servant for the master's household, and through his apprenticeship was gradually given increasing responsibilities. He could become a master after several years' hard work by fulfilling a set of obligations. These included payment of a license fee to the political sovereign, accumulation of enough capital to go into business, an oath to uphold the guild's laws, and the production of a "masterpiece," or example of his craft—a hat by the apprentice hatmaker, a cake by the apprentice baker.

Despite the outward rigidity of its economic system, the Middle Ages proved extraordinarily dynamic and capable of growth. The merchant guilds, formed to represent the purely trading classes, exhibited an aggressive vitality that led to their absorption or domination of the craft guilds that produced the merchandise they sold. Masters in many guilds grew rich and despite the guild regulations succeeded in controlling sizable manufacturing operations.[2]

The outstanding example of this tendency toward big business in a world formally dedicated to small business is the development of the putting-out system of textile production, especially in the wool-cloth manufacturing region of Flanders. Wool cloth was one of the great staples, almost *the* great staple, of medieval long-distance commerce. Technically its production changed little from earlier times until the invention of the spinning wheel in the thirteenth century greatly speeded the production of yarn from fiber. The fibers were first cleaned and carded (combed), then spun into yarn, woven on the hand loom, and fulled

—cleaned, then felted by beating or trampling—and finished (smoothed) and dyed. Rural households that made their own wool cloth skipped the fulling, dyeing, and finishing, and the coarse cloth worn by peasants has been blamed for some of the skin afflictions common in the Middle Ages. But the complete process, resulting in a fine cloth, comfortable for wearing, was not new. What was new in the medieval system was the way the production steps were organized.

Perhaps beginning as a fill-in method of utilizing peasants' time during winter months and other periods when field labor was slack, the putting-out system grew into an urban industry centered in Flemish cities that by the twelfth century had grown large and rich: Ghent, Bruges, Ypres, Arras, Lille, and others. There were many variations in putting out, and the old peasant household production survived in many places, but the great Flemish cloth cities developed a distinct industrial system dominated by a wealthy entrepreneurial class that in many respects foreshadowed the capitalist entrepreneurs of the Industrial Revolution. A sort of pre-industrial revolution was in fact effected by them, in which the craftsmen were subordinated to the control of men who acted solely as merchants and managers of production.

The Flemish wool manufacturer bought his fleece, usually from England, and "put it out" to a weaver, who in his own house, with the aid of his family, spun and wove it into cloth and returned it to the manufacturer, who then either fulled and dyed it in his own establishment or sold it to be finished elsewhere. The form of putting out was a sale and a resale; the manufacturer sold the fleece to the weaver, and the weaver sold the cloth back to the manufacturer. In reality, however, the manufacturer enjoyed a highly advantageous position. He made a profit on the fleece sold to the weaver even if he never saw it again; if war interrupted the flow of commerce he was under no obligation to buy back the weaver's finished cloth, or could buy it back at a low price. Though they worked at home, at their own pace, without being subjected to factory discipline, the weavers were as much at the mercy of the cloth merchants as if they were employees, and it is not surprising that history's first strike was by the weavers of Douai, one of the principal Flemish towns, in 1245.[3]

Yet the putting-out system represented a significant advance in the organization of production. The large quantities of cloth manufactured under it formed one of the main elements in the long-distance commerce between northwest Europe and the Mediterranean that flourished throughout the high Middle Ages. An international division of labor grew up by which undyed Flemish cloth, woven from English fleece, was sold to Italians who took it home to Florence and other cities to be finished and dyed and sold it in the Muslim cities of the Mediterranean. The Florentine wool finishers guild, the *Arte di Calimala*, named for Calimala Street in Florence where the craft centered, became renowned throughout the western world for the beauty and excellence of its products.[4] The craftsmen of Calimala Street did no spinning or weaving whatsoever; the cloth came into their hands already woven, but mere wool cloth, and left Calimala Street a luxury commodity and a work of art. Though Italy itself grew fleece, the sheep of the rocky Italian countryside did not compare with the long-fleeced animals belonging to the great Cistercian monasteries in England's Cotswold hills and Lincolnshire, which supplied the weavers of Ghent and Ypres. The Italians therefore preferred to buy the Flemish cloth, which formed the basis of the great Fairs of Champagne, a year-round international market held almost continuously at one or another of four towns in the French province of Champagne, east of Paris. Thus, medieval Europe's best export was a thoroughly international product involving English shepherds, Belgian weavers, a French trading center, and Italian merchants, dyers, finishers, and navigators.

Other regional specializations developed—arms and armor manufacture at Milan, Toledo, Nuremberg, shoes and leather goods in Cordova and other Spanish cities, copper-utensil manufacture in Dinant (Flanders) and Valencia, silk manufacture in Lucca and Seville, rugs and tapestries at Poitiers and Limoges, harness and saddlery at Paris, Naples, and Barcelona, mirrors and artistic glasswork in Venice.

Under impetus of industrial expansion, the cities of western Europe experienced rapid population growth and many new towns were founded. As medieval historian Pierre Boissonnade said, "A teeming activity transformed the western world as a multitude of artists and artisans created, regenerated, or developed the different varieties of industrial work."[5]

If, apart from putting-out, little in the way of innovation took place in the medieval production system, nevertheless important changes were prepared for the future. For the first time in history, labor-saving devices were actively sought and once discovered, eagerly applied. By the twelfth century waterwheels in dozens of cities were supplying power for tanning, sawing, polishing (armor), crushing (olives, beer mash, metal ore), and operating blast furnace bellows, forge hammers, and grindstones. The most widespread application of the waterwheel, after the grinding of grain, was for fulling wool cloth.

The fulling operation had throughout antiquity been performed either by trampling or beating with a stick. The cloth fulling mill invented in the Middle Ages was a two-fold innovation: wooden hammers replaced human feet, and the hammers were raised for dropping by the power of a waterwheel. One man could monitor the operation of several hammers, simply moving the cloth slowly through the trough.

The Domesday Book of 1086 records 5,000 water mills (waterwheels for grinding grain) in England. Wind power was also vigorously exploited following the introduction of the vertical-sail, horizontal-shaft windmill in Normandy about 1180, an invention evidently made independently of the earlier, less efficient, vertical-shaft mills that had made a desultory appearance in Afghanistan but were little diffused.[6] The windmill vastly increased power resources in the flat lands of northwest Europe, where the fall of streams was slight, where mill dams threatened to flood fields, and where streams froze in winter. By the thirteenth century Ypres, one of the most prosperous of the Flemish cloth towns, had 120 windmills in its immediate suburbs.

Where neither wind nor water could be utilized, the versatile and mobile animal mill operated, a horse or ass walking in a circle to turn a vertical shaft.

The premium put on labor-saving technology led to regarding the organization of work not merely as a convenience, but as a guiding principle, with the rationale that such machinery was beneficial because it saved stultifying drudgery. Though the guilds tended to take a conservative attitude toward technology, they welcomed changes that did not threaten to give an unfair advantage to a few members, or to injure the quality of the product, as when the weavers of Speyer accepted the spinning wheel in 1297 specifying only that it be prohibited in the spinning of warp threads, which needed to be stronger and so could presumably be better made by the old hand method.[7]

As noted in the previous chapter, the Middle Ages witnessed the gradual disappearance of slavery. In the fourteenth century the labor shortage created by the Black Death led to a brief revival of the slave trade, principally to supply domestic servants for the affluent class in Italy, but the institution soon withered. The large class of medieval serfs are not to be confused with slaves, despite the restrictions of the feudal-manorial system that bound them to the cultivation of the soil. They were not owned by their lord, with whom they had a mutual, if somewhat one-sided obligation—the serf's labor service in return for the lord's protection. The principal obligation was that of cultivating the lord's land, perhaps half the manorial domain which the serfs worked in common. In addition, there were such duties as the corvée, or work on roads and bridges, and such obligations as grinding the serf's own grain in the lord's mill (for a payment in kind). Free peasants also worked the land, on conditions very similar to those of the serfs, the main difference in most regions in the later Middle Ages being the peasant's payment of a land rent in return for freedom from the regular labor services.

It was not difficult for a serf to acquire freedom; usually he needed to do no more than go to a town and establish himself as a craftsman—"city air makes one free," was a well-known saying of the medieval towns, in reference to the custom which entitled a serf to his freedom if he lived for a year and a day in a free city. That few took advantage of the opportunity—there was never a problem of "runaway serfs" in the Middle Ages—suggests a general satisfaction with their situation except for specific abuses which in hard times led to uprisings. Given his choice between freedom from his service obligations and more land, the serf would usually have chosen more land. His real enemy—and that of his lord—was the low productivity of medieval agriculture even under the three-field system. Improvement here awaited the new technology and new work organization of a later age.

9. Medieval Engineering, Mining, and Metallurgy

The monumental construction of the Middle Ages showed only slight evidence of the mechanization that affected the organization of work in medieval industry. No technological progress had been made in lifting weights (though an interesting roller conveyor was developed to move them laterally), and the free labor employed never dealt with blocks of stone as mammoth as the eleven-feet-long blocks of the Roman Pont du Gard. Nevertheless, with their smaller stone blocks, the medieval engineers achieved grandeur in scale in their castles, town walls, cloth halls, and above all their cathedrals. One important reason was the invention of the cross-ribbed vault, based on the pointed arch, which—with its engineering companion the flying buttress—made possible the lofty roofs of the Gothic churches and cathedrals.

The organization of work on a Gothic cathedral differed radically from that employed on a Roman temple or Egyptian pyramid. The labor was carried on by professional craftsmen—masons, carpenters, blacksmiths, plumbers (lead workers), bell founders, and glaziers. These craftsmen were armed with a high degree of skill and aided by improvements in tools, notably the wheel barrow. Occasional contributions of volunteer labor by faithful penitents, once thought important, were of insignificant value. The Gothic cathedral was the product of free, hired, and well-paid labor, organized under the direction of an architect-engineer who commanded an excellent salary and enjoyed high social status. Though the names of many have been lost,[1] these master builders were widely known in their own time; for example William of Sens was hired to build Canterbury Cathedral in 1174 on the strength of his reputation.

Besides combining the functions of architect, engineer, building contractor, and work supervisor, the master builder was often an adept sculptor and painter.[2] He designed the molds or patterns used by the masons to cut the stones for the intricate designs of doors and windows, and the wedge-shaped voussoirs for the arches and vaults. He also designed the building itself, usually copying its elements from previous structures on which he had worked or which he had seen in his travels.[3] Though few examples have survived, it is known that he used written plans and sketches, subject to change during the course of construction that often stretched through decades and even centuries. This delay was occasioned by problems of financing, not of work efficiency; where money did not give out, even so vast a cathedral as Chartres could be largely completed in twenty years, while the magnificent Sainte-Chapelle in Paris was built in just thirty-three months. (For comparison, the National Cathedral in Washington, D.C., built on Gothic structural principles but with modern technology, is incomplete after seventy years.)

Not all the work was performed at the site. One crew of masons worked at the quarry, whence the stones had to be hauled by water or by ox-powered transport. The cathedrals' most spectacular feature, the glass, was manufactured in a hut in the forest, where wood for ash was available. The glass was taken to a studio in town for assembly, under the direction of a master glazier who drew the design, or cartoon, on a wooden table, numbering the sections to guide his assistants in cutting and assembling the pieces.

Another typical craftsman involved in cathedral building was the bell founder, actually a brass founder who when not working on church bells fabricated brass pots, basins, and other implements. His technique was little changed from that of the ancient practitioners of his craft—a clay mold constructed around a wax model, the wax melted out and the metal poured in and cooled.

Thus, the outstanding characteristic of medieval monumental construction was craft skill. An even better illustration of the specialization of labor in the Middle Ages may be found in the large-scale metal mining industry that developed in central Europe and whose operation was described in great detail by the physician and geologist Georg Bauer (1494-1555) at the mining center at Joachimsthal. Written under the Latinized form of his name, Georgius Agricola, his classic work, *De Re Metallica*, published in 1556, remained the indispensable textbook for miners and metallurgists for nearly two centuries.[4]

Under the Bergmeister, or master miner, whom Agricola depicts as the chief administrative official at the mine, a whole hierarchy of clerical and technical personnel was employed, and an army of craftsmen specializing in different phases of the mining operation: miners, shovelers, windlass operators, carriers, sorters, washers, and smelters. The mines operated five days a week, around the clock, with the workday divided into three seven-hour shifts separated by an hour allotted for changing shifts.

Animal power was extensively used, with teams of eight horses hitched in pairs to whippletrees to wind windlasses for raising buckets of ore or for drainage. Agricola's numerous illustrations show many types of pumps used: crank-operated, treadmill-operated, and some driven by water power. There were also suction pumps, some simple and some more complex, all requiring specialized craftsmen to operate. The bellows for mine ventilation were operated by human muscle, horses, or water power. Otherwise, most of the mining techniques remained the same as in antiquity. When the ores were brought to the surface they were taken to a sorting table where women, boys, and old men hand-sorted the lumps, putting the good ores into wooden tubs to be carried to the furnaces for smelting, essentially the same process used in the ancient Egyptian and Ethiopian gold mines.

In summary, mechanization in even large-scale enterprises of the Middle Ages was only partial; yet where it could be applied it effectively altered the traditional organization of work, especially in freeing human beings from some of the heaviest labor.

10. Toward the Industrial Revolution: Proto-Factory and the New World

The rapid economic expansion of the tenth to the mid-fourteenth century was violently interrupted in 1347 by the Black Death (bubonic plague), and a decline set in that may have been abetted by other purely economic factors. Recovery was slow, but by the sixteenth century a fresh period of rapid growth was under way.[1] A combination of increased population and increased affluence rapidly enlarged the market and proliferated its demands. Many new products became available, either in response to the demands or themselves stimulating demand. New technology both resulted from and contributed to other advances.

A number of significant innovations in business methods, developed in medieval Italy—commercial credit, double-entry bookkeeping, marine insurance, the transfer of funds by bills of exchange and letters of credit—were by the beginning of the sixteenth century united in a powerful combination that bankers and businessmen could use to forge enterprises on a scale previously unheard of.

A significant philosophical indicator of the new atmosphere was the strong affirmation of the value of work by the leaders of the Protestant Reformation. Luther called work "the base and key to life," while Calvin admonished his followers that thrift, sobriety, and industry in this life were the evidence that one belonged to the predestined elect of the next.[2]

The demographic trend interrupted by the Black Death (which recurred several times with diminishing virulence) was resumed, and even accelerated in the fifteenth to eighteenth centuries. The population of urban centers grew most rapidly: in 1400 only Venice, Genoa, Naples, and Paris had populations exceeding 100,000; by 1700, London numbered 500,000, while Amsterdam, Vienna, Milan, Rome, Hamburg, and other cities had passed 100,000. Such augmented urban populations brought a pressing demand for higher agricultural production. This demand was met not by any marked changes in the organization of work, but by improvements in plant and livestock breeding, improved fertilization practices, new farm equipment, and the introduction of new crops, especially clover, which allowed the highly efficient four-field, or Norfolk, system to supplant the old medieval three-field system. Instead of one third of the land lying fallow all year round, field crops were planted to graze sheep and cattle. Wheat and barley were alternated with turnips and clover, and the system, deriving its name from the region of England where it was pioneered, was copied throughout western Europe and America.

A problem with the Norfolk system was that turnips and other root crops must be sown in rows, cultivated, and hoed. The solution was found once more in a technological advance, the invention by Jethro Tull of the seed drill and the horse hoe. Eventually Tull's new devices and the Norfolk system led to pressure for improvements in other aspects of crop farming to keep up, especially in machines to assist in the heavy labor of reaping the now larger and more numerous crops, but advances here awaited the nineteenth century.[3]

As the new urban middle class created by enlarged commerce grew, the market for what had always been considered luxury goods—comfortable clothing, multi-room houses, pewter dishes and mugs, glassware, cabinets and other furniture, meat, spices, wine—multiplied. Handicraft production under the old guild system was overwhelmed by the demand, and new industrial patterns began to form. Throughout the sixteenth and seventeenth centuries the application of water and wind power to production grew, and the devices to which the old power sources were harnessed became more complex. But far more significant than any technological changes during this period was the development of a new organization of work, designed for large-scale production.

In certain industries the old guild organization had long since lost its original character. Even in the Middle Ages the weavers of Flanders, subject to the putting-out system, were little more than factory workers whose "factory"—their own hovels—was scattered through the town. The proprietors of such "factories" held in their hands the direction of both the production and commercial sides of the business.

The putting-out system gradually appeared in England

in the later Middle Ages, as the country turned from the export of raw wool to the domestic manufacture of cloth. In England putting-out took the form of a rural, or cottage, industry in which the cotter and his wife spun the wool fibers brought by the merchant-entrepreneur from a neighboring town.[4] (In Flanders a similar rustication of the cloth industry also took place through political events; when the dukes of Burgundy acquired Flanders in the fourteenth century, they clipped the independent power of the great cloth cities, which until then had arrogantly enforced their local monopolies of cloth manufacture against neighboring villages.)

In summer, when the man worked in the field, his wife spun; at harvest time everyone worked in the field, and during the winter both husband and wife worked at clothmaking. Spinning and weaving were usually separated by household, the entrepreneur putting out his wool first for spinning and carding, then for weaving, followed by finishing done by other specialized workers.

A significant advance made by the English putting-out system was the abolition of the fiction by which the Flemish weavers had "owned" the wool put out to them. In the English system the cotters understood that they were working on cloth that belonged to somebody else; they were simply employees who worked in their own homes.[5] Working at home had advantages for the worker, who worked at his own pace, not subject to factory discipline. It would be a mistake to overglorify the cotter's relative freedom, however, as nineteenth-century writers, looking back on a vanished era, often did. Evidence is not extensive on the daily life of the cotter and his family, but it reinforces the inference of the basic technology and economics involved: ceaseless hard work for the whole family, scant leisure, poor physical environment in crowded hovels, with piecework pay probably less than what the lowest paid factory workers later earned.

Already by the later Middle Ages the growth of the market was also having a widespread effect on the institution of the guilds. Originally formed to meet the needs of a purely local trade, the guilds were less and less at home in a production apparatus geared to the needs of regional, national, and international markets. The role and function of the merchant predominated over that of the craftsman, a subtle and far-reaching change in the organization of work brought about not by any tools, techniques, or processes of production, but solely by the change in the marketplace. Instead of the craftsman exercising the sales function, as in the old days, the new merchant-salesman began dictating the organization of production. The merchants passed from traders to owners—of material, of tools, of work places.[6]

As they found their power and prestige eroded by the emergence of the new merchant class, the craftsmen of the guilds sought to resist by attaching ever more detailed regulations to their production in an effort to stop the competition of outsiders, particularly from maverick journeymen who set themselves up independently outside town walls and outside the guild structure. The guilds, however, no longer had the strength to enforce regulations, and in time the increasingly powerful national governments began doing so in a broader interest. In Britain, for example, the Elizabethan "Statute of Artificers" of 1563 set down a number of industrial regulations, many relating to such things as apprenticeship, which had for centuries been the domain of the guilds.

The national governments were soon going far beyond

the regulation of craft production in their intervention in economic affairs. In Britain, France, the Netherlands, and elsewhere the state assumed an active, often dramatic, role in commerce and industry. In some countries, notably Britain, the government aided large companies or corporate bodies—wool manufacturers, ironmasters, hatmakers—to achieve larger concentrations of capital and credit through the grants of monopolistic charters. In others, such as France, the government took a direct part in developing industries through state-owned, state-operated enterprises.[7] One of the most famous examples is the Gobelin tapestry works, originally a private enterprise founded in Paris by the Gobelins of Reims, but taken over by the royal power during the seventeenth century and expanded into the foremost tapestry manufactory of Europe. Other royal establishments fabricated furniture, porcelain, and other luxury commodities, especially for the small but rich market of European royalty. Such state-run factories represented two of the essentials of true factory production: the concentration of a large number of workers under one roof, and the imposition of work discipline governing hours and tasks. Yet the Gobelins and the other French royal works were proto-factories rather than true factories. They scarcely altered the division of labor itself. The nature of the products and the limitations of the market dictated hand production, with emphasis on quality workmanship and craft skills. Thus despite their size, the French royal manufactories, which were copied elsewhere in Europe, especially in the porcelain industry, did not possess the third and fourth elements of a true factory system: mechanization and devotion to a mass market. These two elements awaited the eighteenth century.

Meantime, a historical event of great importance began

to make itself felt in the European economy. As is well known, America was discovered twice by Europeans, first in the year 1000 by the Scandinavian Leif Ericson, and second, not quite five hundred years later, by the Italian Christopher Columbus. The significance of the five hundred-year interval is not always appreciated, but European development during this second stage of the medieval period, or high Middle Ages, accounts for the very different effects that followed the two discoveries. Leif Ericson's landing in Labrador had so little result that it hardly left a trace, creating doubt for a long time among modern scholars as to whether it even took place. Columbus' landfall on Watling Island in the Bahamas, on the contrary, led to a swift, decisive, one might say explosive economic development: the exploitation of the American continents and islands by European technology and work organization.

The products of the Far East, especially spices, had played a major role in the medieval European economy because their small volume, high value, and good shipping and keeping qualities made them ideal articles of commerce. They had little effect, however, on European consuming habits. The agricultural products of the New World, on the other hand, had mass impact. Coffee, sugar, and tobacco became major imports, while corn, potatoes, and many other food crops that proved suitable to the European climate enlarged and transformed European agriculture.

Of ultimately greater significance was the suitability of the New World for producing wheat and other ancient Eurasian crops, but European statesmen and opinion makers of the seventeenth and eighteenth centuries were not aware of this. They had clear-cut notions about the new intercontinental division of labor, which they sought to organize in a way beneficial to Europe.[8] The new colonies, they thought, could provide raw materials for the home industries and markets for the resulting manufactured goods. The Spanish colonies shipped silver, hides, sugar, and tobacco in return for clothing, weapons, glass, paper, books, household utensils, wine, and oil. The English forbade their American colonies to export such manufactured articles as hats to Britain, though importing vast numbers of furs to feed the native British hat industry. Lord Chatham threatened that "if America decided to make a horseshoe or a nail I would bring against her the whole power of England."

Perhaps the most momentous single development growing out of the discovery of the New World was the resurgence there of the institution of slavery.[9] The cultivation and especially the harvesting of sugarcane required much onerous labor; and because the harvested cane had to be milled within a few hours of cutting, a plantation system had to be organized. The native population of the West Indies was not numerous enough to supply labor for the huge new market represented by Europe, and furthermore resisted the work discipline imposed. As early as 1518 the Spanish government licensed the importation of 4,000 African slaves into the Spanish American colonies, and the practice was soon followed by the British and French. The British in the West Indies found sugar cultivation so profitable that they devoted nearly all their land to it, importing food from elsewhere.

In the temperate climate of North America, above the sugar belt, slaves were not numerous until the close of the eighteenth century. The fur trapping and trading of French and English Canada, the wheat and corn farming of the New England and Middle Atlantic states, and the agriculture of the Southeast did not depend seriously on slave labor. Even the tobacco fields of Virginia and North Carolina were cultivated mainly by white indentured servants, who arrived from Europe in large and voluntary numbers, working in the fields until they could pay off their indenture, the debt of their passage, and then striking out for themselves in the free land of the West. In 1755 only in South Carolina did Negro slaves represent a majority of the population.

A single technological device, and one of great simplicity, produced a sudden change with consequences reaching far into the twentieth century. Eli Whitney, a young New Englander visiting a plantation in Georgia, learned of the cotton grower's problem of separating the cotton fiber from the seed. In a few days' tinkering he produced a hand-driven machine that pulled fibers through a grid that screened out the seeds. Any blacksmith given a few hours to study Whitney's gin could make one like it, and the South was soon flooded with the new machines. Overnight, cotton growing became highly profitable, and the cotton slave plantation spread across the country from the Atlantic to the Mississippi and beyond.

This immense regional specialization and division of labor assumed a determining influence in U.S. history. It also had considerable effects outside America. In Britain in the years immediately preceding Whitney's invention a series of new devices had revolutionized the textile industry, while the development of a new source of power promised even greater impact. The flood of raw cotton fiber released by Whitney from the American South consequently found a voracious market in the English Midlands, setting in train momentous economic, social, and political reverberations.

II. Work in the Early Industrial Age

11. The Industrial Revolution:
Birth of the Factory

Eli Whitney's cotton gin filled a technological gap that had been created by a series of inventions made in the British textile industry during the previous century. Among many improvements in the loom a decisive one was John Kay's introduction in 1733 of the "flying shuttle," a device that speeded up the operation of the weaver so markedly that the old ratio of four spinners to one weaver was completely upset. Either many more spinners had to be employed or spinning had to be mechanized. The latter goal was achieved by the successive inventions of James Hargreaves, Richard Arkwright, and Samuel Crompton, to such effect that the problem was reversed; even looms equipped with Kay's flying shuttle could not keep up with the supply of thread now available.

In the 1780's Edmund Cartwright succeeded in building a practical loom that ran by water power, and the greatly increased production capacity for wool cloth brought a fresh train of economic and technological consequences. The price of cloth dropped spectacularly and by doing so immensely broadened the market. Cotton, much cheaper to raise than wool, found a new enlarged demand, momentarily baffled by the problem of the cottonseed, but resolved by Whitney's cotton gin in 1793. By 1820 the textile industry of Britain was turning out wool and cotton cloth in a volume undreamed of a few decades earlier.[1] This increased production was both the cause and effect of the factory system.

A contemporary definition of the early British factory system was given by Dr. Andrew Ure in his panegyrical *Philosophy of Manufactures*, "The factory system designated the combined operations of many orders of work people, adult and young, in tending with assiduous skill a series of productive machines, continuously impelled by a central power."[2] Ure's definition accurately identifies some but not all of the essential elements of the factory system. However, the phrase "assiduous skill" distorts the meaning of the new man-machine relationship introduced into the production process by the Industrial Revolution, one of whose prime characteristics was the building of skill into the machine, allowing the use of minimally skilled workers. Further, while implying the organization of work in the phrase "combined operations," Ure did not spell out the importance of the new division of labor imposed by the machines, a change that not only affected the production of goods and the work process itself but had enormous implications for the whole condition of society.

In the old craft guilds, the occupational unit was the individual worker; his job was essentially done by hand, and he usually performed all the operations involved in the production of a single item. The introduction of machines brought a quite different situation. Processes were now broken down into a series of separate operations, each of which was performed by individuals specializing in it. The classic summation of the new technique was given by Adam Smith in the first chapter of *The Wealth of Nations* in his description of a pin factory:

A workman not educated to this business (which the division of labor has rendered a distinct trade), nor acquainted with the use of the machinery employed in it (to the invention of which the same division of labor has probably given occasion), should scarce, perhaps, with his utmost industry, make one pin in a day, and certainly could not make twenty. But in the way in which this business is now carried on, not only is the whole work a peculiar trade, but it is divided into a number of branches, of which the greater part are likewise peculiar trades. One man draws out the wire; another straights it, a third cuts it; a fourth points it; a fifth grinds it at the top for receiving the head; to make the head requires two or three distinct operations; to put it on is a peculiar business; to whiten the pin is another; it is even a trade by itself to put them into the paper; and the important business of making a pin is in this manner divided into about 18 distinct operations, which in some manufactories are all performed by distinct hands, though in others the same man will sometimes perform two or three of them. I have seen a small manufactory of this kind, where ten men only were employed, and where some of them, consequently, performed two or three distinct operations. But though they were very poor, and therefore but indifferently accommodated with the necessary machinery, they could, when they exerted themselves, make among them about twelve pounds of pins in a day. There are in a pound upwards of 4,000 pins of a middling size. Ten persons, therefore, could make among them upwards of 48,000 pins in a day. . . .[3]

Smith's description illustrates many characteristics of the new division of labor. The old handicraft production depended solely upon the workman's skills, to which his tools were simply an adjunct. Now, with the skill built into the machine, production depended on the effective organization of the work force in feeding and operating the machines. The structure of the work process itself changed, and the result was a change in the type of labor demanded.

During the earlier stage of handicraft production, where skill embodied in experience was the prime factor, the traditional progression from apprentice to journeyman to master had corresponded to the needs of a productive economy based upon the skill of the workman. Once the workman became essentially a machine operator, skill gained through experience counted for little. The worker's main task was now reduced to making adjustments for errors in the machinery, feeding it with materials, and checking output to make certain it was performing satisfactorily. In the textile industry, manual dexterity and alert response proved more valuable than experience.

This fact had a serious social consequence, obliquely noted by Ure in his phrase, " . . . workpeople, adult and young." The labor of adult males could be supplanted without loss by that of women and children, whose smaller hands could more easily mend broken threads, while their lesser strength and endurance was more than compensated by wages as little as a fourth or a sixth that of men. Vestiges of the medieval guild apprenticeship lingered, for example, in the seven-year term of apprenticeship, but in a form distorted to suit the new conditions. Children apprenticed in the factory, far from graduating to the rank of journeyman or master weaver, usually found themselves on attaining majority turned out of their jobs. By the 1830's from one-third to one-half of the entire labor force in English cotton mills was under twenty-one, while considerably more than half the adults were women. Ure gives the wage rates prevailing in the Lancashire mills:

> The wages of the males during the period when there is the greatest number employed—from eleven to sixteen [years of age]—are on the average four shillings, ten and three quarters pence a week; but in the next period of five years, from sixteen to twenty-one, the average rises to 10s. 2-1/2d. a week; and of course the manufacturer will have as few [workers] at that price as he can. . . . In the next period of five years, from twenty-one to twenty-six, the average weekly wages are 17s.2-1/2d. Here is a still stronger motive to discontinue employing males as far as it can practically be done. In the subsequent two periods the average rises still higher, to 20s. 4-1/2d., and to 22s. 8-1/2d. At such wages, only those men will be employed who are necessary to do work requiring great bodily strength, or great skill, in some art, craft, or mystery . . . or persons employed in offices of trust and confidence.

To the question of what happened to the older weavers, one

part of the answer lies in the grim demographic evidence that the average life-span of mill operatives was in the neighborhood of twenty-two years.[4]

Wages in the mills were as low as employers could keep them, and employers banded together to keep them low, making agreements to blacklist any weaver who, like Oliver Twist in the workhouse, asked for more. The cost of the new machinery as much as the avarice of the mill owners dictated the policy. The new factory-wage system clashed violently with established traditions of the relationship of work and pay. George Sturt, in *The Wheelwright's Shop*, recalled how as late as the 1880's, when he took over his family's wagon-wheel-making business, "My great difficulty was to find out the customary price" of a given piece of work. "I doubt if there was a tradesman in the district—I am sure there was no wheelwright—who really knew what his output cost, or what his profits were, or if he was making money or losing it on a particular job."[5] Prices in Victorian England—and in contemporary Europe and America —were supposed to be "fair," and wages "just." The new organization of work by the factory system brutally shattered these warm, human, and inefficient concepts and substituted for them the cold, sharp notion of "competition."

· In most factory districts it also shattered the family itself.[6] Though in a few factories whole families were employed as work teams, more commonly the advent of the powered loom destroyed, for better or worse, the family unity of the weaver household. Cottage weaving, with the younger children winding bobbins, older children checking for faults or helping throw the shuttle, adolescents and parents operating looms, had fostered a pattern of family and community life whose knell evoked strong resistance by the weavers until poverty broke down all defenses and the weaving families surrendered their children to the mills. In *The Excursion* (Book VIII) Wordsworth lamented, perhaps excessively, the end of the old rural cottage industry:

> The habitations empty! or perchance
> The Mother left alone,—no helping hand
> To rock the cradle of her peevish babe;
> No daughters round her, busy at the wheel,
> Or in dispatch of each day's little growth
> Of household occupation; no nice arts
> Of needle-work; no bustle at the fire,
> Where once the dinner was prepared with pride;
> Nothing to speed the day, or cheer the mind;
> Nothing to praise, to teach, or to command!
>
> The Father, if perchance he still retain
> His old employments, goes to field or wood
> No longer led or followed by the sons;
> Idlers perchance they were,—but in *his* sight;
> Breathing fresh air and treading the green earth:
> Till their short holiday of childhood ceased,
> Ne'er to return! That birthright now is lost.

The advance of the Revolution was inexorable, and the perfection of the power loom speeded it up. In 1838 there were 2,768 power looms in the important weaving district of West Riding; three years later there were 11,458. The machinery was constantly improved; between 1835 and 1850 the speed of shuttle movements more than doubled, and in 1851 a new power loom wove at twelve to fourteen times the speed of the old hand looms. A low-paid girl, boy, or woman could mind two power looms.

Such machinery could only justify its high cost by continuous operation, making imperative the factory system of organization. The machines' cost also brought a sharp, novel dichotomy in the functions and responsibilities of the participants in the productive process. In the older handicraft production, the artisan had employed his own tools; he was both employer and employee. The new machines were too large to fit into the cottage and too costly for the individual weaver. They could only be owned by the capitalist industrialist, who was also in a position to exploit water and steam power. Hence was formed the new working relationship between employer and employee that Karl Marx called the "wage nexus." The separation of the functions of capital and labor had already come into existence under the putting-out system, in which the capitalist entrepreneur, in effect, owned the materials while the worker owned his tools. But the relationship was now carried a decisive step further. Because the machines had to be kept working on a reliably steady basis, the new factor of work discipline, imposed by the employer but in reality exacted by the machine, was introduced. Here lay a potent source of social conflict.

Even in enterprises not fully mechanized, the advantages of factory discipline were apparent at an early stage of the Industrial Revolution. One of the earliest and most interesting experiments was the pottery works at Etruria, England, designed by Josiah Wedgwood in the eighteenth century "with a view to the strictest economy of labor."[7] Wedgwood laid his plant out so that the ceramic pieces were first formed and then advanced at a continuous progress through the painting room, the kiln room for firing, the account room where the inventory of production was kept, and finally to the storage room to await shipping. Heretofore a pottery worker followed his workpiece from one task to another; in Wedgwood's new set-up the men were assigned a particular post and worked at only one task. Out of 278 men, women and children employed by Wedgwood in 1790, only five had no specialized post. Not only was production volume greatly increased, as in the case of Adam Smith's pin factory, but another improvement became noteworthy, that in the quality of the finished product. Thus the division of labor did not so much destroy the worker's skill as limit it to a particular field of expression, within which it actually increased through repetition.

Wedgwood was consequently one of the first new capitalists to encounter the difficult problem of work discipline. It took all his ingenuity and all the efforts of his supervisors to enforce punctual and constant attendance on his workers. Their old individualistic habits of working at their own pace, taking holidays when they felt like it, "keeping St. Monday," *i.e.*, taking Monday off, and drinking on the job were inimical to the new system. Some of the fines levied by Wedgwood indicate the scope of his managerial problems:

Any workman striking or likewise abusing an overlooker to lose his place.

Any workman conveying ale or liquor into the manufactory in working hours, forfeit 2/—[two shillings].

Any person playing at fives against any of the walls where there are windows, forfeit 2/—.[8]

As an enlightened employer, Wedgwood thought the principles of hard work, sobriety, and thrift which he practiced himself would be beneficial to the workers, but his moral concern was a minor consideration in comparison with the overriding demands of production efficiency. Even for such idealistic employers as Robert Owens, a socialistic paternalism was rooted in the feeling that happy workers would produce more efficiently.

There were not lacking ideologists to defend extreme measures by employers against workers lacking in discipline. One such (J. Smith, *Memoirs of Wool*, 1747) asserted that

> It is a fact well known . . . that scarcity, to a certain degree, promotes industry, and that the manufacturer [worker] who can subsist on three days work will be idle and drunken the remainder of the week. . . . The poor in the manufacturing counties will never work any more time in general than is necessary just to live and support their weekly debauches. . . . We can fairly aver that a reduction of wages in the woollen manufacture would be a national blessing and advantage, and no real injury to the poor. By this means we might keep our trade, uphold our rents, and reform the people into the bargain.[9]

Andrew Ure thought it "nearly impossible to convert persons past the age of puberty . . . into useful factory hands." Such adult recruits, unable "to conquer their listless or restive habits," either quit or were dismissed.

Two qualifying points need to be borne in mind in respect to the new factory working conditions. One is that the picture is spotty rather than completely black—in some cases and places real wages rose. The other is that the hardships of the old putting-out system, though much less advertised, were no less real. Economic security, for example, was no more assured the cotters working at home than it was the millhands in the factory.

Yet it can hardly be doubted that the majority of factory owners exploited their workers mercilessly. The "dark satanic mills" that William Blake denounced spread from Britain to Europe and helped create the oppressed proletariat that rose in protests and insurrections in the nineteenth century. The Sadler Commission, appointed by the British Parliament to investigate working conditions in the early 1830's, recorded testimony indicating a working day for children in the factories lasting fourteen, sixteen, and even eighteen hours.[10] Forty minutes were allowed for the single meal of the day, and half of the forty minutes were usually taken up in cleaning the machines. The foreman, whose wages depended on the output, sometimes brutally beat the children who, toward the end of the day, were too exhausted to take proper precautions against accidents with their dangerously guardless machines. Adults too suffered from the endless repetitive toil, unhealthy and unsafe conditions, and tyrannical foremen, but it was the plight of the children that principally awakened consciences.

Factory conditions—including the proximity into which workmen were necessarily forced—also bred labor movements in all industrial countries.[11] At an earlier stage workers had themselves played a considerable role in the development of machinery. "A great part of the machines made use of in those manufactures in which labor is most subdivided," according to Adam Smith, "were originally the invention of common workmen who, being each of them employed in some very simple operation, naturally turned their thoughts toward finding out easier and readier methods of performing it."[12] But as they perceived the machines as enemies, depriving them of their jobs, the workers turned on them in a naive frenzy. The "Luddites," named for a perhaps fictitious "Ned Ludd," first appeared in Nottingham in 1811. Masked, and operating at night, they destroyed stocking and lacemaking machinery, and were soon imitated by workers in Yorkshire, Lancashire, and other textile regions. Despite some public support, including a famous speech in their defense made by Byron in the House of Lords, the Luddites were crushed by the government, especially through a mass trial at York that resulted in hangings of several rioters and transportation of others. In 1816 the Luddites suddenly reappeared, with riotings beginning again in Nottingham and spreading widely.[13]

Outside England similar riotings took place as workers smashed the machines that they thought were taking away their livelihood. In France the word "sabotage" came into being from the use of wooden shoes (*sabots*) to kick machines to pieces, as French wool finishers rioted in the 1820's. In 1839 Barthelemy Thimmonier, the inventor of the sewing machine, was assaulted in Paris and his machinery wrecked by hand tailors, while in Germany in 1844 the workers staged a revolt later memorialized by Gerhart Hauptmann in his drama *The Weavers*. Even English farm workers attacked new threshing machines in 1830 that threatened their jobs.

Against the inexorable tide of change the Luddites could scarcely hope to prevail, but in some places the riots had the temporary effect of delaying the introduction of machinery. Sometimes, too, machine-wrecking was used as a means of applying pressure on employers, or putters-out, to gain concessions in wages and working conditions. In this sense, Luddism was a sort of collective bargaining by riot. More sophisticated responses by the workers soon developed, and in country after country the long history of the struggle of organized labor began. Here it will suffice to note the observations contained in an "Address to the public" by "A Journeyman Cotton Spinner" of Manchester at the time of an early strike (1818):

First, then, as to the employers: with very few exceptions, they are a set of men who have sprung from the cotton-shop without education or address, except so much as they have acquired by their intercourse with the little world of merchants on the exchange at Manchester; but to counter-balance that deficiency, they give you enough of appearances by an ostentatious display of elegant mansions, equipages, liveries, parks, hunters, hounds, etc., which they take care to show off to the merchant stranger in the most pompous manner. . . . [T]hey are literally petty monarchs, absolute and despotic, in their own particular districts; and to support all this, their whole time is occupied in contriving how to get the greatest quantity of work turned off with the least expense. . . . They are ignorant, proud and tyrannical. . . .

[As for the workers] they have been . . . patience itself—bondmen and bondwomen to their cruel taskmasters. It is in vain to insult our common understandings with the observation that such men are free; that the law protects the rich and poor alike, and that a spinner can leave his master. . . . Where must he go? Why to another. . . . He is asked, where did you work last: "Did he discharge you?" No; we could not agree about wages. Well, I shall not employ you nor anyone who leave his master in that manner. . . .[14]

Yet the most significant effect of the Industrial Revolution from the social point of view was not job displacement or even the hardships of factory life. It was the emergence of the so-called "Social Question," *i.e.*, the creation of the dazzling prospect of an economy of abundance, the question being how to share it. This question was ultimately to give rise to institutionalized means—labor unions and working-class political parties—and socialist ideologies, which together comprised the "Social Movement" of the nineteenth and twentieth centuries, as the working class sought a voice in its own destiny.

As C. P. Snow observed, the Industrial Revolution gave the workers something they had never had before: hope. The abolition of poverty and inequality, it seemed, might be effected by the combination of the new machines, the new organization of work, and the new power source, steam. James Watt's significant improvement of the Newcomen atmospheric-pressure engine, and subsequent improvements on Watt's engine, were to make steam available not only for mine drainage, virtually the sole function of the Newcomen engine, but for the whole range of industrial and transport power needs.

The steam engine itself, and the machine applications to which it gave rise, helped in the rapid development of several other industries, most significantly metallurgy, in which a revolution took place in the early and middle nineteenth century. Wood, the principal material for constructing the simple machinery of the earlier water-powered industry, no longer sufficed and was replaced first

by iron and copper and later by steel. Wood was simultaneously widely replaced as a fuel by coal, especially after the
discovery of the properties of coke by Abraham Darby and
the invention of important new puddling and rolling processes in metallurgy by Henry Cort.

The machine-tool industry, developing at first in Britain
in the first half of the nineteenth century, offered the
prospect of extending the Industrial Revolution to many
more industries, including some not yet in existence. Together with certain other developments, it promised to turn
the mechanization of the English textile industry—whose
proprietors had actually hoped to keep their new technology secret from foreign competition—into a worldwide
revolution reaching into every aspect of production and
extending far into the future.

12. The Coming of Mass Production: The American System

Mass production, the technique of producing large quantities of goods at low cost per unit through a systematic arrangement of men and machines, comprises six recognizable and interrelated elements:

1. Standardization of product.
2. Interchangeability of parts.
3. Precision tooling so the parts will universally fit.
4. Mechanization of the manufacturing process to achieve a high volume of output.
5. Synchronization of the flow of raw materials to the machines and the flow of output from the machine.
6. Continuity, both for the elimination of waste motion and to maintain a smooth flow of materials.

These elements are the basics. In addition, sophisticated mass production requires supervision of standards of quality (quality control), accurate cost accounting, and effective contact with a large-scale market to consume the output. To insure standardization and interchangeability, highly specialized machine tools are necessary. Finally, an organization of work based on a minute division of labor is indispensable.[1]

Mass production was the logical outcome of the Industrial Revolution, the substitution of factory machines for the hand tools of the craftsman, or in the words of philosopher and educator Scott Buchanan, "the progressive passage from 'manufacture' to 'machinofacture.' "[2] The old handicraft operations were broken down into their component parts, with mechanical operations substituted for manual operations. Coupled with the machines were new prime movers, the steam engine, followed by the steam turbine (whose ancestor was the ancient waterwheel), the electric motor and generator, and the gas turbine. The factory, born in eighteenth-century Britain, was the means whereby both men and machines could be organized into larger patterns of systematic operations based on cost efficiency, or, in a European phrase, whereby production could be "rationalized."

In terms of hardware, the essential ingredient for achieving rationalization of production was the machine tool, the machine that makes other machines. Its development in the first half of the nineteenth century was made possible by the advance in metallurgy of the previous half century, during which the steam engine helped produce more iron and also created a demand for carefully fabricated iron parts for its pistons, chambers, and boilers. The value of iron was vastly enhanced by the introduction of machine tools which could quickly and cheaply cut the metal into forms and shapes.[3]

The remote ancestors of the new machines for cutting, shaping, scraping, and grinding hard materials were the primitive awls, knives, gouges, augurs, and scrapers with which early man shaped wood. Over the millennia of the Stone Ages and the centuries of civilization these had evolved into complex mechanisms, the most important of which was the woodworking lathe, an ancient machine that precisely guided a cutting tool to shave away specific portions of the workpiece—table leg, pedestal, chair back. Applied to woodworking as early as Etruscan times, c. eighth century B.C., the lathe was sufficiently perfected by the sixteenth century that clock makers and instrument makers were using lathes to cut brass with an extremely high degree of precision.

Early metal-cutting lathes were used only on small parts, and a considerable advance was necessary to create lathes capable of cutting large parts, especially of iron. The development of the industrial lathe dates primarily from the eighteenth century, an outgrowth and a contributor to the Industrial Revolution.[4]

The first outstanding success was John Wilkinson's boring mill, a lathe that accurately bored the cylinder for James Watt's steam engine in 1775. Watt had conceived his device almost ten years earlier, but among other problems had been unable to find a manufacturer who could produce a cylinder that would keep the steam contained while the piston moved. Matthew Boulton, Watt's partner, was impressed by the accuracy of Wilkinson's mill, which could bore a cylinder so that "it doth not err the thickness of an old shilling." Such a tolerance might not impress modern engineers, but it was remarkable for its time, and helped make Watt's steam engine a practical success.

Another Englishman, however, a generation after Wilkinson, is the true father of machine tools. Henry Maudslay (1771-1831) synthesized the several elements of the new industrial lathe, one by one created for various special purposes, into a general-purpose cutting machine that could hold the workpiece and cutting tool firmly enough to achieve a high degree of precision. Maudslay's machines were the most perfect of their time, and his insistence upon accuracy communicated itself to the entire British machine-tool industry, notably to James Nasmyth (1808-90) and Joseph Whitworth (1803-87), men who produced even more precise and specialized machines.

By the mid-nineteenth century, the basic machine tools—the lathe and its progeny of boring and drilling machines, shapers, and planers—had achieved a remarkable degree of reliable precision, especially after Whitworth's introduction of a standard screw thread. These super-machines were not themselves mass-produced, quite the contrary. No two, even though made in the same shop, were exactly alike. Despite this oddly archaic character, they were well suited for the production of the relatively slow-speed machines of the factories of the day.

Yet the chief development in the third quarter of the nineteenth century took place in America. This was the development of automatic, specialized, high-production machine tools.

Under the influence of contemporary mercantilist economic doctrines, the British government had sought from the mid-eighteenth century to prevent the export of machinery, drawings, models, and even mechanics in a misguided attempt to monopolize the Industrial Revolution. Such legislation could do no more than briefly delay the inevitable spread of the new technology. British machine builders clandestinely sent machines abroad, and British mechanics went with them. A young textile worker named Samuel Slater, for example, memorized the working parts of the new spinning machinery and traveling in disguise, under an assumed name, crossed the Atlantic to found the New England textile industry. But the growth of the Industrial Revolution did not stop with the export of British technology. In both America and continental Europe important new technical advances were grafted onto the original British root-stock.

In America, rich in water power, coal, and other basic resources, a shortage of skilled labor heightened the value of the new concept of "skill built into the machine," while the rapidly expanding market put a premium on mass production.[5] Speed and accuracy of machine production took precedence over elegance of hand manufacture. In the frontier-dominated New World, ancient tradition and custom did not deaden the spirit of innovation. "Yankee ingenuity" became a byword for clever mechanical tinkering aimed at a purely practical result.

Boston merchant Francis Cabot Lowell got the idea of the power loom through personal industrial espionage in Britain, had a machine perfected by the expert New England mechanic Paul Moody, and successfully integrated all stages of textile manufacturing within a single mill complex. Lowell concentrated on a very few, highly standardized, cheap cloths, all woven from a single standard yarn. By 1820, three years after Lowell's death, his Boston Manufacturing Company was running 5,376 spindles and 175 power looms, processing 450,000 pounds of cotton annually. Lowell also pioneered the employment of female labor in the U.S., recruiting teen-age girls from New England farms and housing them in dormitories and boarding houses at the mill site. Of 264 workers employed at Lowell's Waltham plant in 1820, 225 were women and girls, 13 boys, and only 26 men. Thus by effective use of machinery Lowell made a virtue of the American shortage of skilled labor.

By 1834 Lowell, Massachusetts, was established as the most important center of the New England textile industry, with eight large enterprises running a total of 116,000 spindles and 4,000 looms, and employing 6,500 workers, of whom 5,000 were women.[6]

The momentum engendered by Slater, Lowell, and other Yankees did not slacken. Despite Britain's head start in machine production, in the course of the nineteenth century America seized the leadership of the continuing Industrial Revolution through the creation of what came to be known as the "American system" of manufactures.[7]

The American system has been defined as "a method of manufacture in which complex mechanical devices were produced in a series of sequential machine operations." It involved the making of large groups of exactly identical parts—"interchangeable parts"—that could be fitted together to form machines or other devices. Its technical requirements included mass manufacture, the use of power machinery especially designed for the work to be done, and gauges to insure uniformity through precision.

Although the American system did not really originate in the United States, it achieved its fullest development there. American nationalist historians long attributed the invention of interchangeable parts to Eli Whitney, but it has been established that a number of continental Europeans anticipated Whitney, who, for that matter, was only one of a number of Americans to expound the idea. Christopher Polhem of Sweden used elements of interchangeability as early as the 1720's, and by the 1790's the method was widely discussed; a French gunsmith, known to history only as M. Blanc, described it to Thomas Jefferson, among others, though it is not certain that he applied it in practice. In the first decade of the nineteenth century the technique was applied with dramatic success by the French emigré engineer Marc Brunel, who later built the world's first subaqueous tunnel, to the manufacture of pulley-blocks for the British navy. Working with Maudslay, the pioneer of machine tools, Brunel installed a set of 44 machines in the Portsmouth Navy Yard that carried out a sequence of operations starting with the raw materials of wood and ending with the finished pulley blocks. Brunel's arrangement permitted ten men to make 160,000 pulley-blocks a year, a task that had proved beyond the capacities of the 110 men formerly assigned.

Brunel's performance made surprisingly little impression on British industrialists, but the situation was otherwise in America. Early in 1798 Whitney contracted with the United States government to make 10,000 rifles in twenty-eight months, an undertaking undoubtedly based on machine-produced interchangeable parts. Whitney apparently was thinking mainly in terms of utilizing unskilled labor, but his effort was not completely successful since he took several years to fulfill his contract.[8] Nevertheless, Whitney, his Connecticut neighbor Simeon North, Roswell Lee at the Springfield Arsenal, and Captain John H. Hall at the Harper's Ferry Arsenal were all using powered machinery to produce interchangeable parts for small arms by 1820, and their example inspired other U.S. industries.[9] By the 1830's the concept had spread to factories producing, among other things, New England's famous clocks and watches.

The world did not become fully conscious of the new

development in the U.S. until the Crystal Palace Exhibition in London in 1851. After viewing the American exhibit of machines used to produce identical interchangeable parts, British industrialists sent engineering missions across the Atlantic to study the technique of their young rival, and soon after the British government went so far as to order American machines installed in Britain's Enfield arsenal. What particularly impressed such Britons as Whitworth, the leader of the British machine-tool industry, was the array of special-purpose machine tools developed by the Americans. Of 131 machines purchased by the British, 51 were milling machines, a new type of lathe that represented the first important original American contribution to machine-tool design. In the milling machine, the rigid single cutting edges, which operated in the old lathes like firmly held chisels, were replaced by rotary cutters, resembling cog wheels with sharp teeth. Milling machines permitted work to be done much more quickly and with much less heating of the tools and workpieces. The first milling machine had been designed in 1848 by Frederick W. Howe, in Windsor, Vermont, to be used in the manufacture of the famous Sharp's breech-loading rifle. Sharp's partner, Joseph R. Brown, produced the first universal milling machine, capable of all kinds of spiral milling, gear cutting, and other metal work previously done by the laborious and expensive hand method.

Brown also improved the grinding machine to the point where it could be used to shape metal, rather than merely to polish or sharpen. In the grinding machine the need was for precision combined with an adequate speed of rotation and a durable abrasive for the grinding wheel. Brown provided the precision, and better abrasive wheels were presently developed by Swen Pulson in Worcester, Massachusetts, and patented by Pulson's employer, F. B. Norton.

Another improvement in machine tools was the turret lathe, which mounted a series of cutting tools so arranged that they could be brought successively to bear on the workpiece. A skilled operator could set up the tool so that semi-skilled workmen could operate the machine repetitively and perform six or eight formerly specialized machine operations rapidly and accurately.

By the end of the third quarter of the nineteenth century, the American system was turning out textile machinery, sewing machines, and a host of other industrial products. The fundamental industrial sector of working and shaping metals had now undergone a complete transformation. Hand tools were almost universally replaced by machine tools operated by semi-skilled workers, vastly accelerating production and lowering costs.

The preeminence of American industry in standardization and interchangeability of parts formed the indispensable basis for the next great stage of the continuing industrial revolution, the assembly line. The gasoline-powered automobile was a European invention, but mass production of the automobile developed, by no accident, in the United States. Although the assembly line is forever associated with the name of Henry Ford, the ultimate in precise interchangeability of parts was achieved by Henry M. Leland, founder of the Cadillac Motor Car Company. Leland insisted on the most rigorous standards of uniformity for every component of his cars.[10] In 1908 an exhibition of the American technique in England drew widespread notice. Leland's British distributor had three Cadillac cars taken apart at the Royal Automobile Club's test track, caused the parts to be piled up and scrambled, and had 90 parts chosen at random by club officials to be discarded and replaced from stock. The three Cadillacs were then re-assembled and performed faultlessly in a 500-mile test run.

By that time machine tools had opened the way for the transformation of the organization of work, by building the skill into the machine, by making precise interchangeability possible, and by permitting the breakdown of the work process into component parts. The American system was now ready to take on its twentieth-century form.

13. Henry Ford and the Moving Assembly Line

The mechanization of production, the standardization of parts, and the application of power made mass production a fact in certain industries such as textiles. In certain others, one more feature remained to be added: the continuous flow of materials through a series of machines.

Conveying systems for the handling of materials can be traced to antiquity. The Greeks used screw conveyors; the Assyrians, bucket elevators. From ancient Athens we have records of a ceramics factory in which vases were lined up on a long table alongside which the workers moved to paint stripes on the vases, a sort of reverse assembly line. The principle of the belt conveyor was familiar to Leonardo da Vinci, and the idea of the roller conveyor for moving heavy weights can be seen in medieval manuscripts dealing with or showing building construction. In his book describing mining and metallurgical processes, Agricola shows bucket elevators used to raise water from mines.

A striking early example of the assembly-line principle is medieval Venice's famed arsenal, where war galleys were fitted out by hauling them through a channel lined with warehouses. As the galley passed, cordage was passed from one window, provisions from another, arms from another, "and so from all sides everything that was required, and when the galley had reached the end of the channel all the men required were on board, together with the complement of oars, and she was equipped from end to end," reported a fifteenth-century observer. "In this manner, there came out ten galleys fully armed, between the hours of three and nine."[1]

A significant advance in manufacture by assembly line was the water-powered grist mill built near Philadelphia in 1785 by the American inventor Oliver Evans.[2] Grain was fed in at one end of the mill and, by a system of conveyors and chutes, passed through the various stages of milling and refining, to emerge at the other end as finished flour. Evans' system was widely imitated in other milling factories, and the idea of continuous-flow processes was introduced into other industries.

Francis Cabot Lowell, the pioneer of the power loom in the New England textile industry, also introduced the principle of flow production in his Waltham mill. In Lowell's plant design, the flow was vertically upward. The water-wheel (power source) and machine shop were in the basement; carding equipment (for combing the fibers) was on the first floor; spinning machinery was on the second, weaving on the third and fourth.[3]

The Fourdrinier machine, invented in France in 1799, produced paper in a continuous roll, and by 1835 printing on such a continuous roll had become feasible. The technique of processing a moving product was soon introduced into canning, brickmaking, and sugar refining.

Most of these early applications of continuous processing did not involve doing mechanical work. Furthermore, they seemed more a matter of convenience in handling than a rational effort to increase production. The true assembly line did not evolve until late in the nineteenth century. It appeared, rather surprisingly, in the American meat-packing industry centered in Chicago and Cincinnati.[4] In the slaughterhouses, short overhead trolleys had long been used to shift the heavy carcasses from worker to worker. When someone thought of connecting the trolleys with chains to form a continuous line, and of powering the line to move the carcasses at a steady pace, the true assembly line was born, even though its effect might better be described as a "dis-assembly line." Each worker necessarily concentrated on a single repetitive task, and unnecessary movements of either workers or materials were automatically restricted. The trolley's speed, arbitrarily regulated, now determined the rate of productivity, which at once increased radically. In his autobiography Henry Ford explicitly credited the origin of the moving assembly line to the meat-packing industry: "The idea in a general way came from the overhead trolley that the Chicago packers used in dressing beef."

When Ford came on the scene all the elements of assembly line technique were thus present, and Ford had to invent nothing really new. Yet it was Ford's genius (abetted by some bright subordinates, such as Charles E. Sorensen and Clarence W. Avery) that synthesized all the elements in an amazingly effective combination for the mass production of perhaps the most complex form of manufactured goods ever produced, the automobile.[5] Ford's perfected assembly line changed the course of history, first in the United States, then elsewhere.

Ford was not the only manufacturer to conceive of the automobile as an item of mass consumption. Another who did so—by no coincidence also American—was Ransom E. Olds, whose one-cylinder "Merry Oldsmobile" was the object of a vigorous attempt to rationalize production with a technique not far removed from the assembly line.[6] By organizing his labor force into gangs and controlling the flow of materials, Olds achieved an output of 5,000 cars a year in 1904, a figure considered remarkable. But apart from the difficulties inherent in mass-producing a highly complicated mechanism, Olds was defeated by another basic difficulty, namely, the inadequate quality of his product. Olds—and several other American manufacturers on the same track—put too much effort into production speed (and therefore economy) and not enough into design of a product that would meet the demands of the market.

Henry Ford recognized this problem clearly, and found a brilliant solution to it. His Model T Ford—the immortal "flivver" or "Tin Lizzie"—appeared in 1908. Visitors to automobile museums have often been surprised to find that the 1908 Model T was not, by the standards of its day, a small car. What it was, rather, was mechanically simple, a quality which helped it to achieve two great basic requirements of the mass driving public: durability and economical operation.

The next step was to insure a selling price that would reach the mass market. Ford calculated such a price as $600, and was proved correct when in 1912 the Model T was sold at this figure and production could not keep up with demand.

Now the stage was set: The right product design had achieved mass-market acceptance. The year 1913 witnessed the culmination of Ford's sustained efforts. On May 1 of that year Ford first experimented with a moving assembly line for producing magnetos (generators). The conventional method of magneto manufacture was to present each workman with a pile of 29 parts; when he had completed assembling them into a magneto he was given—or went and got—29 more parts. "With one workman doing a complete job," Ford noted, "he could turn out from thirty-five to forty pieces in a nine-hour day, or about twenty minutes to an assembly." Ford put 29 men in a line and assigned each of them one of the 29 operations. Each had a pile of units of the part he was to add. As the assembling workpiece, hand-pushed on rails, arrived at his station he added his part and it was pushed to the next station. This primitive, unpowered assembly line at once reduced assembly time from 20 man-minutes per magneto to 13. Powering the line (and raising it to a height of optimum convenience, an interesting early correction), reduced the time to five man-minutes.

The success of the magneto operation was promptly followed up by adaptation of the moving line to motors and transmissions. The crankcase, which had previously been carried by a series of laborious steps to the paint tanks and thence to the motor assembly, was now picked up by a conveyor belt that bore it through a paint tank and a drying oven to the assembly line. Chassis assembly, dash assembly, front-axle assembly lines were soon established. Under the old system where the parts for each chassis were brought to a fixed station, assembly required 12-1/2 man-hours per car. In August, 1913, Ford tried hauling the chassis past stockpiles of components, a distance of 250 feet, with six assemblers moving along with the chassis. The method cut the labor time in half, reducing total assembly to less than six man-hours. Power was next applied through a chain drive, and the assemblers given stationary locations while the chassis moved past them. Profiting from the magneto experience, Ford next positioned parts and work stations at heights to minimize stooping and facilitate handling. By the end of April, 1914, the assembly time was reduced to 93 man-minutes—an eighth of what it had been.

The final logical step was the integration of all production into a single huge assembly line, into which parts and sub-assemblies flowed like tributaries into a river and from the mouth of which rolled an endless succession of Model T Fords. "Every piece of work in the shop moves," Ford exulted. "It may move on hooks on overhead chains going to assembly in the exact order in which the parts are required; it may travel on a moving platform, or it may go by gravity, but the point is that there is no lifting or trucking of anything other than materials." Cars came off the line at the fantastic rate of one every two minutes, a time which was later halved.

The quite unbelievable total of more than 300,000 Model T Fords was produced in 1914, and more than 500,000 in 1915. In 1923 and 1924 output reached nearly 2,000,000 cars annually, and the unit price dropped with the increase in sales. A statistic that remains incredible in the annals of industrial economy is that in 1924, when a Model T touring car sold for $290, more than half of all the automobiles on the roads of the world were Model T Fords.[7]

Ford had succeeded spectacularly in bringing together the separate features of the assembly line process, with the result that in order to keep up with the rate of final assembly of the chassis, similar assembly-line techniques had to be instituted elsewhere in the automotive industry. Parts suppliers began converting to the assembly line. As in the case of the interchangeable part concept, the technique spread rapidly to other industries that required an assembly of parts into a final product—refrigerators, washing machines, sewing machines. Mass production of appliances, as with automobiles, made possible lower prices but did not (necessarily) reduce quality, and it created for the first time the possibility of a mass-production, mass-consumption society.

The assembly line puts a premium on the division of labor, indeed, on the organization of the entire work process. The assembly line for the chassis of an automobile illustrates what Karl Marx called the "heterogeneous" division of labor, wherein complete parts are fitted to other parts. Adam Smith's illustration of a pin factory demonstrates what has been called the organic division of labor, meaning that the same object is gradually transformed through a succession of distinct operations. This might also be accomplished by assembly line, as in the case of the Ford magneto assembly. In both types of division of labor the tasks are broken down by division and subdivision as minutely as possible to the point where their performance requires virtually no skill, or at least to where the needed skill is readily acquired. The simpler the task, the easier it is to hire a worker to perform it and the less training he requires, thus lowering labor costs while speeding up the work.

The economic consequences of the fragmentation of work seemed to be wholly favorable, certainly from the employer's point of view.[8] Voices had long been raised in protest, however, over an aspect of the new system. Among the earliest and most heeded were those of Alexis de Tocqueville, John Ruskin, and Karl Marx. The French political observer, the Victorian aesthete, and the Communist theoretician were in agreement on the moral results for the worker of the new definition of his function. "When a worker is unceasingly and exclusively engaged in the fabrication of one thing, he ultimately does his work with singular dexterity," wrote de Tocqueville in *Democracy in America*, "but at the same time he loses the general faculty of applying his mind to the direction of his work. He becomes every day more adroit and less industrious; so that it may be said of him that in proportion as the workman improves, the man is degraded."[9]

"We have much studied and much perfected, of late, the great civilized invention of the division of labor," wrote Ruskin in *The Stones of Venice*, "only we give it a false name. It is not, truly speaking, the labor that is divided; but the men:—divided into mere segments of man—broken into small fragments and crumbs of life so that all the little piece of intelligence that is left in a man is not enough to make a pin or a nail, but exhausts itself in making the point of a pin or the head of a nail."[10] Marx, while recognizing the economic advantages of the factory system, pointed out the physical and moral damage which the worker was bound to suffer, damage he attributed not to the technology of machine production but to the capitalist economic organization of it. Under capitalist industrial conditions, with the worker employed by an employer who owned his place of work and his tools, "work is external to the worker," who in Marx's eyes, "has a feeling of misery, not well-being, does not develop freely a physical and mental energy, but is physically exhausted and mentally debased. . . . The alienated character of work for the worker appears in the fact that . . . in work he does not belong to himself but to another person."[11] Approaching the problem later from still another direction, the American economist Thorstein Veblen stressed the "instinct for workmanship," which he considered as a universal human trait and which he feared was endangered by assembly-line production methods.[12]

Interestingly, even Adam Smith had considered that the industrial worker's condition demanded government regulation of some sort:

> The uniformity of [the worker's] stationary life naturally corrupts the courage of his mind. It corrupts even the activity of his body, and renders him incapable of exerting his strength with vigor and perseverance in any other employment than that to which he has been bred. In every improved and civilized society, this is the state into which the laboring poor, that is, the great body of the people, must necessarily fall, unless government takes some pains to prevent it.

The assembly line increased the stresses that de Tocqueville, Ruskin, Marx, Veblen, and Smith perceived even before its advent. Its march was inexorable. It dictated the pace of the worker's job. Its continuous movement forced every worker in the factory to perform his specialized task in the brief time allotted before the piece on which he was working was carried to the next work station. To the tedium of performing the same small task in the same way all day long was added the nervous strain of performing it within an arbitrarily fixed time. That time was fixed not by the worker himself but by the factory management. If management wanted to speed up output to meet an unexpected market demand, it simply increased the pace.

This formidable new capacity of management became

the focal point of bitter controversy between assembly line workers and assembly line employers. Thus, although the assembly line represented a major step forward in the rationalization of production, that is, in producing goods by the most efficient and economical technique, it raised a momentous question of social relations between the employing and working classes.

14. The New Division of Labor: The Discipline of the Machine

In our yard, at half-past eight a.m., Aunt Arlie McVane, a clever, kind-hearted, but awfully uncouth, rough sample of the 'Ould Sod', would make her welcome appearance in the yard with her two great baskets, stowed and checked off with crullers, doughnuts, ginger-bread, turnovers, pieces, and a variety of sweet cookies and cakes; and from the time Aunt Arlie's baskets came in sight until every man and boy, bosses and all, in the yard, had been supplied, always at one cent a piece for any article on the cargo, the pie, cake and cookie trade was a brisk one. Aunt Arlie would usually make the rounds of the yard and supply all hands in about an hour, bringing the forenoon up to half-past nine, and giving us from ten to fifteen minutes 'breathing spell' during lunch; no one ever hurried during 'cake-time.'

After this was over we would fall to again, until interrupted by Johnnie Gogean, the English candyman, who came in always at half-past ten, with his great board, the size of a medium extension dining table, slung before him, covered with all sorts of 'stick', and several of sticky candy, in one-cent lots. Bosses, boys and men—all hands, everybody—invested one to three cents in Johnnie's sweet wares, and another ten to fifteen minutes is spent in consuming it. Johnny usually sailed out with a bare board until 11 o'clock at which time there was a general sailing out of the yard and into convenient grogshops after whiskey; only we had four or five men among us, and one apprentice —not quite a year my senior—who used to sail out pretty regularly ten times a day on the average; two that went for whiskey only when some one invited them to drink, being too mean to treat themselves; and two more who never went at all.

In the afternoon, about half-past three, we had a cake-lunch, supplied by Uncle Jack Gridder, an old, crippled, superannuated ship carpenter. No one else was ever allowed to come in competition with our caterers. Let a foreign candy-board or cake basket make their appearance inside the gates of the yard, and they would get shipped out of that directly.

At about five o'clock p.m., always, Johnnie used to put in his second appearance; and then, having expended money in another stick or two of candy, and ten minutes in its consumption, we were ready to drive away again until sundown; then home to supper.[1]

This eyewitness picture of the casual work discipline in a mid-19th century New York shipyard is not unique. A New York cigar manufacturer complained: "They [his workers] come down to the shop in the morning; roll a few cigars and then go to a beer saloon and play pinnochio or some other game . . . working probably only two or three hours a day." Coopers, who candidly protested the introduction of barrel-making machinery not on the grounds that it threw them out of work, but simply because it "took a great deal of joy out of life," had the custom of knocking off work entirely on Saturday, their pay day:

Early on Saturday morning, the big brewery wagon would drive up to the shop. Several of the coopers would club together, each paying his proper share, and one of them would call out the window to the driver, 'bring me a Goose Egg,' meaning a half-barrel of beer. Then others would buy 'Goose Eggs,' and there would be a merry time all around. . . . Little groups of jolly fellows would often sit around upturned barrels playing poker, using rivets for chips, until they had received their pay and the 'Goose Egg' was dry.

Saturday night was a big night for the old-time cooper. It meant going out, strolling around town, meeting friends, usually at a favorite saloon, and having a good time generally, after a week of hard work. Usually the good time continued over into Sunday, so that on the following day he usually was not in the best of condition to settle down to the regular day's work.

Many coopers used to spend this day [Monday] sharpening up their tools, carrying in stock, discussing current events, and in getting things in shape for the big day of work on the morrow. Thus 'Blue Monday' was something of a tradition with the coopers, and the day was also more or less lost as far as production was concerned.

'Can't do much today, but I'll give her hell tomorrow,' seemed to be the Monday slogan. But bright and early Tuesday morning, 'Give her hell' they would, banging away lustily for the rest of the week until Saturday, which was payday again, and its thoughts of the Goose Eggs.[2]

The picture is strikingly reminiscent of that drawn by an observer in the English textile mills of an earlier age, when "St. Monday" was sometimes followed by a St. or half-St. Tuesday, and when according to tradition the loom went in the early part of the week to the easy pace of "Plen-ty of time. Plen-ty of time," and only toward the week-end clacked to the swifter "A day t' late. A day t' late."

Such long-established work habits, growing out of centuries-old life-styles of European craftsmen, and brought to America by the wave of nineteenth-century immigrants, soon ran afoul of the new industrial age. Owners, managers, and foremen bullied, threatened, and swore over them, while on a higher level preachers, politicians, and publicists engaged in a strenuous crusade extolling honest toil as the noblest of virtues. Calvin's admonition to work hard to accumulate wealth but not to spend it on one's self was distorted into a religious principle of work for work's sake and the abhorrence of idleness and pleasure. The new ideal was by no means limited to America. European workers heard it preached too. In Britain, Andrew Ure declared that workers should perform their tasks as a "pure act of virtue . . . inspired by the love of a transcendent being . . . . Where shall mankind find this transforming power?—in the cross of Christ."[3]

But it was in labor-short America that the cult was most fanatically proclaimed. Against the old free-and-easy work habits symbolized by Arlie McVane and the "Goose Eggs," it had scant effect beyond convincing employers of their own righteousness and their workers' sinfulness.

Then came the assembly line. A worker could argue with a foreman or deceive a boss. He could slip out for a drink, a smoke, a snack, or a game and make up for it later. But he could not slip out from a moving assembly line and come back to make it up. The line demanded his presence every minute from starting time to quitting time, and not only his presence but his attention. Loafing, resting, frolicking, socializing were banished. The line was inexorable.

A new kind of worker, living in a new relationship with his raw materials and his tools, had been created. A military discipline was automatically imposed in defense of the systematization of the new production mode. The machine imposed its rhythm on the work process, and the pattern of work included the worker himself. He became a component of the machine.

From the point of view of management, the continuous flow of raw materials, the time discipline imposed by the machine, and the need for standardization and quality control exacted the utmost care in supervising each step of production.[4]

In a sense, the factory system merely brought into manufacturing the organization of work that had long been applied to large-scale construction and mining. Since prehistoric times, whenever men had sought to make something requiring the work of more than a single individual, there had been need for some form of production organization. Slaves required a taskmaster who in turn required an overseer, while a clerical specialist to keep track of costs was needed to show how the job was going. Thus was born the rudimentary organization of management.[5] The factory extended this ancient hierarchical system of management, making it much more complex, with significant impact on the relationship between worker and manager.

In the old handicraft organization a man was apprenticed early in life to his life trade, and as age and experience brought superior skill his status was enhanced. That relationship between skill gained by experience and status of the worker vanished with the introduction of the factory system; indeed, age became a handicap rather than an advantage if it brought a decline in the worker's reflexes and coordination.

At the same time that the worker was experiencing a degradation, a rapid proliferation of managerial and white-collar personnel was taking place. Mass production demanded accurate cost accounting of the entire manufacturing process, and, in a free-enterprise economy, mass sales produced by a mass sales force. Thus, three large new classes of workers appeared on the industrial scene:

Supervisory. The great increase in scale brought an extension of the "authority line" from workers supervised by their employer to workers supervised by sub-foremen, foremen, department heads, shift superintendents (the high cost of the machinery made two or three shifts desirable or mandatory), factory superintendents, and plant managers. In giant corporate organizations that operated many plants there were divisional managers, vice-presidents in charge of production, and other executives.

Staff. The complexity of large-scale production, especially in the light of the increasing reliance upon machinery and the synchronous flow of materials to, within, and from the plant, required the development of "staff" organization as well as "line" organization. The staff consisted of expert professional specialists—accountants, engineers, chemists, and many others. Although not directly involved in the production process, their work was essential to keeping the production line going, maintaining the flow of raw materials in and finished products out, and insuring the quality control and accurate cost accounting requisite to economic operation.

Sales. To assure the flow of products from the mammoth factories to the consumer, a trained and organized sales force was indispensable. Here again a hierarchy of supervisory personnel was necessary.

Thus a tremendous elaboration of supervisory control was brought about by the assembly line.[6] Failure of any workers on the line to follow their instructions and perform their specialized tasks within the time allotted threatened a breakdown of the whole production process. At the same time close coordination of the different stages of the process was necessary to guarantee smooth flow of materials and continuity of manufacture. Finally, foremen and subforemen were required to set up the machine and the job, and to assure that basic work standards were met.

Henry Ford conceived the idea of carrying the rationalization of production a final step farther. He proposed a gigantic multi-stage plant in which every component of an automobile would be produced, from raw materials to the finished product. His River Rouge (Detroit) plant was an ambitious attempt to achieve this ideal. Iron ore was to be brought directly to the plant, smelted and rolled; other raw material was to be shipped in for primary processing and manufacture of components. A glass factory would provide plate glass. Great economies, Ford thought, could be made by efficient coordination of the production process in such an integrated plant, saving the need to stock large inventories and store large supplies of materials. Everything would flow continuously from raw materials to finished automobile.

But although Ford actually built the River Rouge plant and largely carried out his ideal of completely integrated production—and though the model was much admired throughout the world, and still functions efficiently—Ford's example this time was not widely followed. The economics of materials transportation and certain new technical developments made it unnecessary and in some ways undesirable to attempt such complete integration. Other automobile manufacturers, notably General Motors Corporation, found that their needs could be better supplied by independent producers of component parts than by producing everything within their own organization at a single point of manufacture.

The economics of plant-to-market transportation also dictated dispersal. The Ford company itself soon moved to establish branch assembly plants throughout the country in order to lower transportation costs of the finished vehicles to the consumers. The meat-packing industry that had given birth to the assembly line found it desirable to move from the giant centers in Chicago, Kansas City, and Cincinnati to local plants throughout the U.S. Technical developments made the dispersal of production units in other industries economically preferable. The old waterpowered plants, such as the New England textile mills, required sites where water flowed swiftly. Steam-powered plants were drawn to the source of steam power's raw material, coal.

But electric power, the product of mainly European research and development in the middle and late nineteenth century, but first fully exploited by Thomas A. Edison in the United States, had the wholly novel characteristic of being transportable over long distances with slight loss. Generated at a central plant and carried by wire, electric power could be converted at a factory located anywhere to a form suitable for machine operation.[7] Small plants, located near modest but exploitable markets, were now practicable. Conversely, a factory could now be located near a raw material source. Electric power made it possible to optimize a plant's location in respect to whatever the ruling economic constraints were.

Improvements of the technology of communication also facilitated dispersal. Efficient administration required extensive record-keeping for inventory control, routing of raw materials and finished products, and communications among the disparate elements of the production process. The development of telephone and teletype communications meant that branch organizations dispersed throughout the country could be controlled and supervised by a central office which might be entirely separate from any production facility. The size and location of the productive units were thus freed from the demand for face-to-face communication within the managerial organization, just as they were freed from the requirements of the steam-power plant. Management by remote control became the order of the day. Corporate management in, for example, New York, could control production hundreds and thousands of miles away.

Still another effect of the new mass production was to heighten the tendency toward an international division of labor. In *The Wealth of Nations* Adam Smith had eulogized the new division of labor, still only local, in glowing terms:

It is the great multiplication of the productions of all the different arts, in consequence of the Division of Labor, which occasions in a well-governed society, that universal opulence which extends itself to the lowest ranks of the people. Every workman has a great quantity of his work to dispose of beyond what he himself has occasion for; and every other workman being in exactly the same situation, he is able to exchange a great quantity of his own goods for a great quantity, or, what comes to the same thing, for the price of a great quantity of theirs. He supplies them abundantly with what they have occasion for, and they accommodate him as amply with what he has occasion for, and a general plenty diffuses itself through all the different ranks of society.[8]

Seventy-three years later (1859), in his inaugural lecture as Regius professor of modern history at Oxford, Goldwyn Smith expanded the earlier Smith's point to include the growing international division of labor. The second, Victorian Smith grew absolutely lyrical:

The laws of the production and distribution of wealth are . . . the most beautiful and wonderful of the natural laws of God, and through their beauty and their wonderful wisdom they, like the other laws of nature which science explores, are not without a poetry of their own. Silently, surely, without any man's taking thought, if human folly will only refrain from hindering them, they gather, store, dispense, husband, if need be against scarcity, the wealth of the great community of nations. . . . They call on each nation with silent bidding to supply of its abundance that which the other wants; and make all nations laborers for the common store; and in them lies perhaps the strongest natural proof that the earth was made for the social being, man. . . . It would be an exaggeration to erect trade into a moral agency; but it does unwittingly serve agencies higher than itself, and make one heart as well as one harvest for the world.[9]

There was at least no doubt that mass production increased the interdependency of the world. Mass production demanded an enormous supply of raw materials, whose dispersion over the face of the globe necessitated international trade, while it turned out quantities of finished goods that the local market could not consume. The market grew regional, national, and finally international. Mass production thus created an interdependence of the entire world that in theory might have brought a lessening of international tensions. In actual fact it had rather the reverse effect, as the industrial nations sought to insure the supply of raw materials necessary for the functioning of their factories and the appropriation of colonial markets to consume their products.

In relation to the worker, this stage of the Industrial Revolution, consisting of the super-mechanization of production through the assembly line, has been described by a modern scholar as having two main effects. Georges Friedmann, a French industrial sociologist, has written:

Mechanization leads to a simultaneous and contradictory dual evolution: on the one hand, subdivided tasks increase in number, bereft of initiative and responsibility, and of overall views. This is the 'de-spiritualization' of work. On the other hand, there appear ... preparatory tasks, tool-making, supervisory work, work in the construction of complex machines, which require training. Much more than this, work ... in which, as a result of mechanization, the operation on material has become separated from the worker's hand, no longer required speed or strength of execution, but precision and attention; that is, not quantitative but qualitative characteristics. The quality of work in this case shows the worker's ability. Thus, the process of de-spiritualization and re-spiritualization of labor accompany one another.

Though admitting that the new factory technique in most cases brought more "de-spiritualization" than "respiritualization," Friedmann insists that there is "no rigorous determinism in either of those evolutions. . . . [T]he choice itself depends on the socio-economic milieu in which the evolution takes place."[10] Support for Friedmann's contention can be found in data that show a reversal in more recent times of the trend that marked the earlier stage of industrialization when the number of skilled workers dropped rapidly and the number of unskilled rose proportionately. As machines have begun completely to replace unskilled workers, the proportion of skilled workers has risen.

Friedmann is writing from the historical plateau of the later twentieth century. In the early years such an insight was hardly possible. Yet Prince Kropotkin, the benign Russian revolutionary intellectual of the 1900's, observed that "precisely in proportion as the work required from the individual in modern production becomes simpler and easier to learn, and therefore also more monotonous and wearisome—the requirements for the individual for varying his work, for exercising all his capacities, becomes more and more prominent." Prince Kropotkin's solution, to integrate work instead of subdividing it, was a remarkable foreshadowing of the job-enrichment programs of the 1970's. (See Chapter 20).

15. The Mass Production Farm

Although the development of mass-production agriculture has taken place largely in the middle decades of the twentieth century, it is convenient to describe its growth at this point in our narrative because it is related closely to the kind of mass production developed in industry early in the century as much as to more recent industrial trends. It has reached its highest technical development in the United States, though it is also conspicuous, though not as uniformly successful, in the Soviet Union, Canada, Australia, and certain other advanced agricultural countries.

In the early nineteenth century North American agriculture was practiced on family farms employing the techniques and organization of work that had characterized farming for many centuries. The work group was the family, with cooperation among neighbors during harvesting. Despite some improvements in tillage techniques and farming implements, such as the plow and seed drill (planter), output remained fairly static. Nearly three-fourths of the American labor force was employed on farms, as compared with six percent in the 1970's. One farmer could produce the food and fiber to meet the needs of only three or four city dwellers, compared with forty in the 1970's.

Rapid advances in agricultural technology took place through the nineteenth century, even without serious changes in the organization of farm work.[1] At the beginning of the century, 100 bushels of corn required 344 man-hours of labor; by World War I the figure had dropped to 147 man-hours. Yet despite its increased productive capacity the American family farm was already in a decadent state, and the huge units sometimes called "agribusinesses," specializing in a single crop and profiting from factory-type managerial techniques, were beginning to appear, especially in the western and southwestern U.S. Early in the nineteenth century animal power supplanted human muscles for many heavy tasks; for example, horses on treadmills drove threshing machines. The power revolution in all its stages was accompanied by new mechanical devices,[2] of which the most notable was Cyrus McCormick's reaper, which immensely facilitated grain harvesting, the most labor-consuming of all agricultural tasks. Another important new device was John Deere's steel plow, whose steel mouldboard was capable of turning the rich soil of the Midwest that had stuck stubbornly to the old wooden mouldboard.

Out of McCormick's horse-powered reaper grew the combine, a machine that not only reaped the grain but bundled and tied it. Late in the century steam power took over from horses, to be in its turn supplanted by internal combustion power and, for some purposes, electricity.

Mechanical harvesters for non-cereal crops began to appear, eventually including machines capable of handling such difficult or delicate crops as cotton and tomatoes.

Still other improvements came in techniques for clearing, draining, and irrigating farmland. In addition, better and more intensive use of fertilizers developed, especially as chemical technology learned to make synthetic fertilizers from nitrogen in the air. The chemical industry also developed pesticides to protect plants from insect enemies and diseases. Perhaps the most important area of scientific advance was in plant genetics, which early in the twentieth century brought hybrid corn and, later, new varieties of wheat. The new plants gave much larger yields because they were better suited for particular soils, more hardy, and more resistant to insect attack and plant disease. With the increase in mechanical tillage and harvesting came the development of plant breeds especially suited to machine handling. By the middle of the twentieth century, productivity advances based either on genetics or on more intensive use of fertilizer were accounting for an estimated two-thirds of the increased crop production per acre in the United States. Equally important, if less spectacular, were gains derived from improved breeding of livestock.[3]

Another source of the improved productivity of agriculture lay in food technology, mainly in the conversion of raw foodstuffs into finished products through such processes as milling, cleaning, sorting, separating, and grading. The long-established preserving process of canning was put on a mass-production, assembly-line basis, as was, somewhat later, the newer process of freezing, further stimulating the transition from the small family farm to the huge, specialized corporate farm. These vast transformations in American agriculture might not have been possible without the aid of a major social invention, the land-grant college with its agriculture research station and extension services, which fostered scientific and technical improvements and brought them to the farmer.[4]

A few figures illustrate the size of the surge in agricultural output.[5] The corn, oat, and barley yield in the U.S. increased nearly sixfold from 1850 to 1950. Cotton, which had yielded 150 pounds per acre since the Civil War, felt the impact of chemical fertilizers and mechanization beginning in the late 1930's, and in the next thirty years climbed to above 500 pounds per acre. Milk production per cow virtually doubled between 1925 and 1965. Laying hens, which had averaged about 130 eggs per year in 1940, increased their output by the 1960's to 220.

An insight into the mechanization that contributed so much to these increases is given by the average investment of over $21,000 per worker in U.S. farms. Capital investment on the larger farms, up to 10,000 acres, runs to $165,000 per worker. Tractors, after replacing horses in the first quarter of the century, grew larger and more powerful (from a 30-horsepower average in 1945 to 62 in the 1970's) and were equipped with attachments not only for plowing and harvesting, but for the application of fertilizers, herbicides, and insecticides. The mechanical tomato harvester, developed in the 1950's, permits a crew of workers to gather a harvest amounting to a ton of tomatoes per worker per hour. To achieve such production, a variety of tomato was bred that had a thicker skin to resist bruising, and that would ripen uniformly, so the fruit could all be harvested at once.[6]

All these revolutionary changes powerfully affected the organization of work in agriculture. Yet the work patterns of industrial mass production could not simply be borrowed wholesale. In a factory the same technique can be repetitively employed on an assembly line, shift after shift all year round. In agriculture, tasks change cyclically with the seasons. At a certain time of year the ground must be prepared for planting; later it must be cultivated, and still later the crop must be harvested. The organization of farm work also varies from farm to farm. Thus, farm workers cannot be given the same degree of specialization that is possible in industry. On the family farm a diversity of crops are still grown by traditional farming practices, the family work force engaging in a constantly changing round of tasks. In the Western cattle ranches the nature of the tasks—riding the range, herding, and branding the cattle—reserved them for professional cowhands. More recently the old style of open-range ranching has given way to gigantic feed lots, where cattle can be scientifically fattened. Along the Pacific coast specialized one-crop farming is used to raise apricots, cantaloupes, lettuce, walnuts, lemons, oranges, grapes, and other fruits and vegetables with maximum efficiency. Some of these still require hand picking. Migratory farm workers still follow the crops northward during the picking season, but it seems only a question of time till technology solves the problem of harvesting even these fragile crops.

The organization of work in cotton growing has also been affected by mechanization in the form of the cotton picker and other aids. In the antebellum South, plantations averaged 200 acres with eight slaves, six as field hands and two in the household. In the aftermath of the Civil War an attempt was made to maintain the plantation system by substituting wage contracts for slavery, but this soon gave way to the sharecropper system, by which a tenant farmer raised the crop and divided it, generally fifty-fifty, with the landowner, who usually supplied seed on credit and paid half the cost of fertilizer and ginning. The mechanical cotton picker made rapid inroads on this system by eliminating the need for hand labor. In the late 1940's, one man with a mule could plant, cultivate, and pick an acre of cotton in 160 hours working time. In the 1970's, machine planting, cultivating, and harvesting of an acre are accomplished with only thirteen and a half hours of labor. In the Mississippi Delta, where some 30,000 seasonal workers were employed in the backbreaking task of cotton picking as late as 1960, the introduction of machinery had by 1967 reduced the number to 7,225, picking the same amount of cotton.

By the 1970's other technological elements were affecting cotton farming in almost pendulum-like fashion. At the beginning of the decade synthetic fibers had improved to the point where they threatened almost entirely to supplant cotton—despite the popularity and some advantages of blended cottons and synthetics. However, when the "energy crisis" reduced the petrochemical feedstocks available for synthetics, the demand for cotton soared.

Corn and wheat are perhaps the field-farm processes most amenable to factory production methods. Mechanization now monopolizes planting, cultivating, and harvesting of corn, which is scarcely touched by human hands. In wheat farming, the farms are even larger and the mechanization is even greater. Two peak seasons—seeding and harvesting—represent about five-sixths of the year's work. At harvest time a mechanized crew is paid a fee for harvesting the crop. A modern combine crew numbers five men and performs an array of tasks that early in the century required 26—boss, engineer, and two firemen for the steam tractor, separator tender, derrick boy, roustabout, two cooks, three hoe-down men, a sack-jig man, a sack sewer, two drivers, two loaders, and eight leader box wagon drivers.

Of all modern farm operations, however, dairying and poultry-raising have proved susceptible of the highest degree of factory-type organization. Unlike other branches of agriculture, these do not represent seasonal products with a planting-harvesting cycle, but a daily work pattern endlessly repeated as in industry. On the dairy farm, there is little specialization of tasks; the same workers feed and tend the cows, milk them, and clean milking machines and containers. But production of chickens for meat exhibits virtually all the characteristics of the modern automated factory. In these "chicken factories" a computerized feed-bin determines the exact quantities of mixed foods for a healthy diet and quick growth, mixes the chicken feed, and delivers it automatically to the cage where the chicken is confined throughout its life. The proper amount of water is also delivered automatically, and waste is periodically removed by mechanical means. When the chicken reaches the right weight for processing, it is automatically killed, plucked, and cleaned on an assembly-line basis. The result has been an astonishing increase in productivity and reduction in the unit cost per pound of chicken. In the seventeenth century Henry IV of France expressed the hope of seeing the day when there would be a "chicken in every peasant's pot on Sunday." That hope was realized in nineteenth and early twentieth-century Europe and America. But even as late as the 1950's few foresaw that chicken was soon to become the cheapest meat available in the U.S., a major source of protein in the American diet.

The "chicken factory" involves high capital investment and therefore has become the province of large companies, some of which control all aspects from producing feed through processing and selling—often including cooking and serving through franchise chains.

The capital investment demanded for such highly mechanized and even automated farming operations is entirely out of the reach of the traditional American family farm. A relatively small number of large farms—less than a fifth of the total of U.S. farms—now produce three-fourths of the farm products marketed, while at the other end of the scale some million and a half small family farms account for only five per cent of agricultural sales. The small farmer, not in a position to take real advantage of mechanization, or even of new seeds, fertilizers, pesticides, and other advances in farm technology, has been placed in a difficult, if not hopeless, competitive situation.

The application of mass-production techniques to agriculture has not met with equal success everywhere. The optimistic hopes of the Soviet regime embarking on the First Five-Year Plan in 1927 were dashed by the resistance of the peasants to the organization of collective farms, and since then the Russian leadership has had numerous disappointments, especially when it compared agricultural with industrial progress. By the 1970's it was evident that agriculture simply is not susceptible to the dramatic type of increase in industrial output achieved by the First and subsequent Five-Year Plans. Nevertheless, Soviet agriculture has made substantial progress, contrary to much opinion in the outside world and to many expressions within the Soviet press.[7]

Soviet farms are divided into two classes, state farms and collective farms, distinguished from each other mainly by the fact that on the collectives each family is permitted to cultivate a small plot of land of its own apart from the main farm holdings, while the state farms are meant to be run simply as agricultural factories. The distinctive organizational feature of Soviet farming has been the Machine Tractor Station, a regional distributing center that owns and operates most of the machinery used on the farms. In a way the Machine Tractor Station resembles the contract harvester of the American western wheatlands, taking over responsibility for harvesting the crops of a number of farms that would find it uneconomical to maintain such large machine fleets individually. The Machine Tractor Stations, however, also function as coordinating and supervisory units representing the central authority in checking on farm operations. The organization of work at the stations is divided between a staff that maintains and services the machinery and one that operates it on the farms.

In the 1970's a trend was evident in the Soviet Union toward enlarging the size of farms to a point where self-sufficiency in machinery would be economically justified.

An interesting contrast with the Soviet agricultural aim is that of Japanese agriculture.[8] Instead of encouraging production of large, powerful tractors that can only be used effectively on very large farms, the Japanese government, which plays an important role though hardly that of the Soviet government in national economic decisions, pushed the development of small tractors suitable for the rice-paddy cultivation of Japanese family farming. In both the Soviet and the Japanese cases it is evident that technical and material considerations were mingled with political and social ones in decision making.

The United States government has also been forced to intervene in agricultural economics, but perhaps in a less positive way than the Japanese and certainly in a far more negative way than the Soviet. The largest development in U.S. agriculture, with implications that have proved revolutionary far beyond the borders of the farm, has taken place with scarcely any encouragement or intervention by the government. The mechanization and rationalization of agriculture, completely altering the scale as well as the nature of farming, have for better or worse, virtually deruralized America. Farm workers and potential farm workers flooded the cities just as changing industrial technology was eliminating a great proportion of the unskilled jobs in industry.

To follow this second development, it is necessary to return to the industrial scene of the late nineteenth century.

III. Modern Production: Technology and Consequences

16. The Science of Mass Production: Frederick W. Taylor and the Worker as a Machine Component

At the dawn of the twentieth century, the ongoing surge of mass production was regarded as a natural outcome of social evolution. The coalescence of minutely subdivided work processes into a smoothly operating industrial machine seemed in accord with Darwin's discovery of biological evolution and the concepts of social progress derived from it by Spencer, Durkheim, and others. The division of labor seemed part of a universal design whereby specialization of function would lead to a harmonious reconciliation of the whole.

Finally, the moving assembly line, with its demand for synchronization of many different elements in a continu-

151

ous process, implied a higher degree of social cooperation than any of man's productive tasks in previous history. Its outpouring of material goods and creature comforts seemed hardly short of miraculous.

According to Henry Ford, "The key to mass production is simplicity." Three principles, Ford believed, underlay this simplicity:

a) The planned, orderly and continuous progression of the commodity through the shop;

b) The delivery of work instead of leaving it to the workmen's initiative to find it;

c) An analysis of operations into the constituent parts.

These are distinct but not separate steps. . . . All three fundamentals are involved in the original art of planning a moving line production.[1]

The theory Ford enunciated was designed for automobile production by assembly line, but his principles (especially his third point) were susceptible of a much broader application. Even before Ford, a very similar approach had been taken by another engineer, no less remarkable than Ford himself, who conceived of a general rationale for all industrial work, a set of theoretical principles that would optimize efficiency on any job. Frederick Winslow Taylor's audacious and imaginative efforts led to the foundation of an entirely new field of study, the scientific analysis of work itself, which came to be called Industrial Engineering. Through industrial engineering the managerial function—planning, coordination, and supervision—was elevated to a paramount position in the production process.

As a youth, Taylor[2] had planned a career at the bar, and had prepared for Harvard Law School, but an illness interfered and as part of his recuperation his doctor prescribed manual labor. Taylor went to work first for a pump manufacturing company, and later for the Midvale Steel Company in Philadelphia, and discovered his real vocation. Night study gained him a degree in mechanical engineering from Stevens Institute of Technology in 1883, and the following year he became chief engineer at Midvale. Meantime, as a foreman, Taylor had been struck by the bitter antipathy of the workers—"I walked home at night with an apprehension of a sudden attack in the dark"—an antipathy he had no difficulty tracing to the character of the foreman's job, which entailed endless, day-long driving of the men to keep working, to work harder, to stop loafing. It occurred to him that this hostility might be alleviated by an improvement in the efficiency with which the men did their work, that is, that they might be taught to perform their jobs with less effort, and so be enabled to earn more pay for increased output.

Such an improvement in the efficiency of the individual worker would obviously redound to the company's profit. Increased production was also in the interest of the consumer; Taylor envisioned a gateway to an industrial Utopia that would shower blessings on worker, manager, and public. The gateway, he thought, was an optimization of the worker's time and energy.

In the Midvale plant he observed that workers had widely varying ways of performing the same job. Some were clearly using their muscles more efficiently than others. Taylor reasoned that if each man's work were as logically ordered as were the actions of the machines, a marked improvement in production would result. The task of management, he concluded, should be to ascertain the best way to do the job, to provide the correct tools, and to train the worker to act in accordance with precise instructions. Finally, the worker should be provided with an incentive. Though Taylor believed in the widely popular piecework system of contemporary industry, he saw that the real question of compensation, from the point of view of optimizing efficiency, was motivation, that what mattered was not exactly how the worker was paid or even exactly how much, but that, in the worker's mind, a relationship should be established between the efficiency of his working technique and the size of his pay envelope.

Taylor took his ideas to the Midvale plant management. Youthful though Taylor was, he had already demonstrated a mechanical aptitude verging on genius, with several inventions to his credit (eventually he secured more than a hundred patents, including an extremely important one for hardening tool steel), and his superiors decided to let him experiment. Over the next few months he studied nearly every element in the productive process of the plant, including tools, plant layout, and the role of management, but his emphasis was on the individual worker. Taylor observed how each worker did his job, determined the basic motions necessary—lift, turn, push, bend, etc. He then analyzed these to identify the essentials and the nonessentials. Besides rewards for increased production, the worker was promised ample rest periods.

Some tasks being done by the Midvale workers, Taylor discovered, were not properly part of their job, for example, taking time to sharpen cutting tools. This "down time" he eliminated by assigning tool-sharpening to a special crew who did the work on a continuous basis.

When each job was rationalized and the worker trained,

Taylor timed him with a stopwatch. The worker was then issued an instruction sheet detailing exactly how he was now expected to perform his job, giving the time allotted to each operation, the motions to be employed, the tools to be used. "What I demand of the worker," Taylor said, "is not to produce any longer by his own initiative, but to execute punctiliously the orders given, down to their minutest details."[3]

A vivid description in Taylor's own words of how he put his theory into practice is drawn from his experience at Bethlehem Steel, which hired him in the 1890's:

'Now, Schmidt, you are a first-class pig-iron handler and know your business well' [he told a strong but untrained worker]. 'You have been handling at a rate of twelve and a half tons per day. I have given considerable study to handling pig iron, and feel sure that you could do a much larger day's work than you have been doing. Now don't you think that if you really tried you could handle forty-seven tons of pig iron per day instead of twelve and a half tons?'

[Skeptical but willing] Schmidt started to work, and all day long, and at regular intervals, was told by the men who stood over him with a watch, 'now pick up a pig and walk. Now sit down and rest. Now walk—now rest,' etc. He worked when he was told to work, and rested when he was told to rest, and at half past five in the afternoon had his forty-seven tons loaded on the car. And he practically never failed to work at this pace and do the task that was set him during the three years he was at Bethlehem; and throughout this time he averaged a little more than $1.85 per day. . . , 60 per cent higher wages than were paid to other men who were not working on the task work. One man after another was picked out and trained to handle pig iron at the rate of forty-seven tons per day until all of the pig iron was handled at this rate. . . .[4]

One of Taylor's most famous experiments came to be known as the "Science of Shoveling," a name originated by derisive enemies, but one which Taylor proudly flaunted in discussing his lifework before a Congressional committee in 1912. Each laborer at Bethlehem, he recalled, had brought his own shovel to the yard and used it to move all the different kinds of material.

> We would see a first-class shoveler go from shoveling rice coal with a load of three and a half pounds to the shovel to handling ore from the Mesabi Range, with thirty-eight pounds to the shovel. Now is three and a half pounds the proper shovel load or is thirty-eight pounds the proper shovel load? They cannot both be right. Under scientific management the answer to this question is not a matter of anyone's opinion; it is a question for accurate, careful, scientific investigation.

Taylor's solution was to design his own shovels and supply them to the men. He progressively reduced the handle length of the shovel designed for the heaviest material, the iron ore, and steadily increased the daily output until he found the optimum handle length. Ultimately he provided the men with a variety of fifteen different shovels, each designed to move a certain type of material, ranging from short-handled flat shovels for iron ore to broad, scoop-shaped shovels for the light rice coal.

This was not all. Taylor also sent a team about the plant

training the workers in the science of shoveling. He enter-
tained the Congressmen with an elucidation:

> There is a right way of forcing the shovel into mater-
> ials . . . and many wrong ways. Now, the way to shovel
> refractory stuff is to press the forearm hard against the
> upper part of the right leg just below the thigh, like
> this, take the end of the shovel in your right hand and
> when you push the shovel into the pile, instead of using
> the muscular effort of the arms, which is tiresome,
> throw the weight of your body on the shovel like this;
> that pushes your shovel in the pile with hardly any
> exertion and without tiring the arms in the least. Nine
> out of ten workmen who try to push a shovel in a pile of
> that sort will use the strength of their arms, which
> involves more than twice the necessary exertion.[5]

In his conception of a scientific approach to the problem
of industrial production, Taylor undoubtedly made what
Harlow Person called "a meaningful and fundamental
break . . . with the past." A basic element in the system was
the time study, designed to "find out how quickly the various kinds of work that went into the shop ought to be done."
Though Taylor wavered somewhat in his view of which
workman should be timed, saying on one occasion, "Select a
good, fast man," and on another, "Give me an average,
steady man," he finally settled on a formula that involved
timing several different men "who are especially skillful,"
on the theory that such men, once trained, would earn
markedly higher pay and so provide an object lesson to the
rest. The motions of these men, and the tools they used,
should be examined, and a stopwatch used to time each of
their basic movements. All "false movements, slow move-

ments, and useless movements" should be eliminated, and the remaining "quickest and best" movements collected and imposed, along with the best tools.

Some of Taylor's reforms fitted into an ongoing trend throughout industry that was steadily eroding the formerly all-encompassing authority of the shop foreman by placing such elements of production as recording of costs, ordering of materials, scheduling of jobs, and storage of finished parts in the control of office-managerial personnel. In the Taylor system supervisors in the plant's front office were given the task of devising routine for each job. They wrote instruction cards for the workmen, prepared time and cost cards, and through a "shop disciplinarian" insured that the workers cooperated. A "gang boss" made certain that the workers had the proper tools and materials and that there were no delays, a "speed boss" oversaw the work, an "inspector" checked the product, and a "repair boss" kept the machinery in top condition.

Taylor was not entirely alone in his concepts even at an early date. In the French steel industry a similar rationale of industrial work was independently conceived by Henri Fayol, though with different emphases.[6] The Bolsheviks under Lenin planned to develop a socialist version of Taylorism, but the exigencies of the First Five-Year Plan led them to postpone the effort—as it turned out, till after World War II. Thus, it was only in America, with its rapidly growing industrial plant, that Taylorism took serious hold. By the time of his death in 1915, Taylor had many disciples, who organized the Society to Promote the Science of Management, later called the Taylor Society. Among the most prominent were Henry L. Gant and the noted husband-wife engineering team of Frank and Lillian Gilbreth.[7] The

Gilbreths, who helped make the term "industrial engineering" known to the general public, gained added renown at a later date when Frank Gilbreth, Jr., wrote a best-selling book about the home life of their large family, *Cheaper By the Dozen*, in which his father's passion for optimizing all kinds of work processes was humorously recalled. The Gilbreths' field of special interest was "motion study," and their most famous job experiment was dramatic improvement in one of the most ancient craft traditions, the art of bricklaying. Gilbreth wrote Taylor about his discovery:

> My God. . . . Think of it! Here I am a man weighing over 250 pounds, and every time I stoop down to pick up a brick I lower 250 pounds of weight down two feet so as to pick up a brick weighing 4 pounds, and then raise my 250 pounds of weight up again, and all of this to lift up a brick weighing 4 pounds.

The Gilbreths devised an adjustable scaffold that improved the average bricklayer's performance from 120 bricks an hour to 350. To designate the irreducible time-motion unit of any work task Gilbreth coined the word "therblig," an anagram of his own name.

The term "scientific management," to describe the whole Taylor system, was popularized chiefly by Louis D. Brandeis, later a Supreme Court justice, in arguing as a lawyer before the Interstate Commerce Commission. Brandeis used Taylor's management theory to prevent a threatened railroad rate increase by showing that the railroads could increase their profits more by adopting efficient management policies than by raising their rates.

Scientific management, or "Taylorism" as it was also

commonly called, had special characteristics when applied to assembly line production.[8] These can be reduced to a set of six:

1. A mechanically controlled work pace (the moving assembly line).

2. Repetition of simple motions.

3. Minimum required skill, judgment, or experience, and therefore minimum required training.

4. Operating procedures predetermined, with tools and techniques selected for the worker.

5. Subdivision of the product, so that the worker perform his task on only a small fraction.

6. Superficial attention required of the worker, enough to keep up with the moving line.

The combination of the six factors made the worker "an interchangeable part of an interchangeable machine making interchangeable parts."

Taylor and his disciples assumed that workers desired to be utilized efficiently, to perform their work with minimum effort, and to receive more money. Scientific management therefore promised to make the worker happier and more satisfied with his job.[9] Because it promised to do this, the worker was expected to welcome having not only his physical movements but his thought processes standardized. There was one correct way to do a job, and only one, and that one best way was determined by the requirements of the machine process.

This conviction of Taylor and his followers proved to be their Achilles' heel. Experience has shown that there is actually not "one best way" to do most jobs, that the "one best way" is best only for the particular worker who finds it best. Workers vary in age, size, strength, and other physical characteristics, even without taking account of the wide range of psychological differences that affect their approach to a job.

Taylor of course was not oblivious to the fact that workers had feelings. But he tended to discount them. "In the past," he wrote, "the man has been first; in the future the system must be first." He thought workers would be happy if they would only give up their stubbornness and do things the way he taught them. An inefficient worker to Taylor was "a bird that can sing and won't sing." An English admirer, a little carried away by Taylor's evangelism, likened him to Christ:

> He went up to men . . . that he saw humdrumming along, despising themselves and despising their work and expecting nothing of themselves and nothing of anyone else and asked them to put their lives in His hands and let Him show what could be done with them.[10]

Taylor, like Phileas Fogg, counted his steps in his walk to and from his office, not with the object of insuring stable continuity but with that of discovering the most economical route. He designed his own tennis racket to help win the national doubles championship in 1881. He pioneered nonbutton, slip-on shoes to save time. In a word, he was a fanatic, and his own psychological makeup blinded him to the relevance of workers' human feelings to their job performance.

This aspect of Taylorism, its refusal to allow room for workers' subtler motivations, bred job dissatisfaction in Taylorized plants. Further, some employers inevitably ignored the altruistic elements in Taylor's system and used the time-and-motion studies simply to set unrealistically high norms of production, speeding up the pace of the assembly line while keeping wages down. In a situation where the worker perceived that the fruits of his improved performance accrued only to management, deep resentment developed, reinforced by the negative psychological reaction inspired by the basic nature of Taylorism.[11]

In the decade after 1910, when scientific management was being applied wholesale in American industry, labor opposition arose. The speed-up of assembly lines brought protests, absenteeism, sabotage, strikes, and an impetus toward union organization. Management fought back with its traditional weapons of propaganda, coercion, blacklisting, and scabs. The unions enjoyed some successes, notably in forcing the United States arsenals to outlaw the stopwatch used in time studies, along with Taylor-advocated bonus and premium plans.

By the time of Taylor's death in 1915 it was evident that while scientific management could indeed spawn remarkable improvements in efficiency of production, it failed to fulfill its inventor's hope of benefiting the worker. By fragmenting the work task, Taylorism simplified the job but made it more exhausting. Instead of lightening labor it increased fatigue and often caused physiological and neurological damage. The worker on the assembly line was chained to the pace of the line, while Taylorism completed the job of robbing him of his ancient sense of identification with what he was producing. Taylorism amounted to a misuse of the human tool, and to the consternation of the new "industrial engineers" it frequently resulted in poor quality of work and lowered productivity.[12]

In a word, the concept of Mechanical Man, like Adam Smith's Economic Man, proved too limited.

"The essential flaw" in Taylor-type efficiency methods,

as Peter F. Drucker has pointed out, is that "the worker is put to use as a poorly designed, one-purpose machine tool, but repetition and uniformity are two qualities in which human beings are weakest. In everything but the ability to judge and coordinate, machines can perform better than men."

The new microworker, especially when assigned to the assembly line, found himself a minute and anonymous part of a gigantic work process that made it impossible for him to relate his own task to the finished product.

The prophecy of Emile Durkheim was fulfilled:

> If the individual does not know whither the operations he performs are tending, if he relates them to no end, he can only continue the work as a matter of habit. Every day he repeats the same movements with monotonous regularity but without taking any interest in them, and without understanding them. . . . One cannot remain indifferent to such debasement of human nature.

One of the handicaps under which the Taylor disciples labored was the fact that they inevitably approached their problems from the standpoint of management.[13] This may help explain why, when a new approach came, it was supplied not by the industrial engineers, but by social scientists, and resulted in the foundation of another new discipline: industrial psychology.

17. The Hawthorne Effect: Elton Mayo and Industrial Psychology

In 1924 the Hawthorne Works, located in a suburb of Chicago, was the scene of a series of experiments in industrial environment whose original intention was quite modest. The Hawthorne Works was the principal plant of the Western Electric Company, the manufacturing arm of the Bell Telephone system. It employed 30,000 workers, both male and female, to mass-produce telephonic equipment. The labor required was unskilled or semi-skilled, and the characteristics demanded were speed and dexterity in carrying out simple, repetitive assembly of components. The reason for the study was an observed tendency to fatigue on the part of workers who were, by the standards of the day, very well treated, with a 48-hour workweek, good pay, a pension plan, and recreational facilities. Western Electric was considered to be an enlightened employer, and the Hawthorne factory environment comparatively good.

The aim of the experiments was to identify favorable or optimum conditions of production in respect to a range of environmental factors, including pay, hours, work breaks, fringe benefits such as hot lunches, and lighting conditions. Workers were asked to volunteer participation.

The study was under the direction of Elton Mayo, an engineer who had recently studied problems of fatigue in a Philadelphia factory. Mayo and his team began with experiments using the new control-group technique. Two groups of employees making the same telephone component under identical conditions were enlisted, and the general aim was explained to them. For the experimental group the shop lighting was improved, while for the control group it was left as it had been. The expected result was obtained, a modest increase in production by the experimental group. But to the confoundment of the investigators, the control group also increased production, and by virtually the same amount.

Further experimentation only deepened the puzzle. When illumination was either increased or decreased production rose. Even when the workers were told that the light was to be increased and it was left unchanged, production rose, and the workers even stated that they liked the "increased" illumination.

Mayo realized that he had stumbled onto something far more significant than any findings that might have been made about illumination. By good luck, he was the kind of honest (and curious) investigator who does not ignore or cover up unexpected results, but pursues them.

Mayo persuaded Western Electric management to enlarge the scope of the experiment. A group of young women assembling telephone relays were chosen, and for a brief period a record was kept of their production without the women's knowledge. It was ascertained that under "normal" conditions they produced 2,400 relays a week. The women were then put on a piecework pay basis. Production of relays rose. Next, rest periods were introduced. Production again rose. Rest periods were lengthened, free lunches provided, and the workday shortened by an hour. Production rose once more. Changes in lighting, humidity, and temperature brought further improvements. Finally, conditions were returned to exactly what they had been at the beginning of the experiment. Instead of declining, production now reached the record level of 3,000 relays a week.

From early in the experiment, Mayo had arranged to have the women workers consulted on proposed changes, and their comments encouraged. They were given veto power over any changes, and were told to work at a natural pace and not try to push themselves to satisfy the experimenters. Finally, they were given permission to do the work in their own particular way, without the standardization of movements which had long been imposed by the time-and-motion studies of the industrial engineers. A startling effect was an 80 percent decline in absenteeism. Medical checkups showed the women to be in good health, free of evidence of the fatigue that had prompted the studies in the first place.

Studying the reports on the conversations between his researchers and the women, Mayo slowly figured out the explanation. The women found the experiments enjoyable. They liked sharing their ideas with the investigators, and were especially gratified by the feeling that the experiments they were acting out could lead to improvements in working conditions for all the workers. These positive attitudes were stimulated not by physical improvements in working conditions brought about by the tests, but by the tests themselves. In asking their help and cooperation, the investigators had unwittingly given the women an important signal—that they had special value, and that their opinions as well as their physical well-being mattered to the company. This improvement in work performance resulting from an improved psychological attitude became known to social scientists as the Hawthorne Effect.

The Hawthorne experiments were at once greatly extended, becoming the largest series of studies made up to that time not only in industrial psychology but in the entire field of sociology. Over 21,000 workers were interviewed, and it was clearly established that giving the worker a chance to express his opinions improved his attitude toward his work. Many other discoveries were made. The labor force at Hawthorne was found to be composed of a number of informal groupings, constituting a whole sub-culture with its own customs, which not surprisingly were often at variance with the purposes of management. Social scientist Stuart Chase, reviewing the Hawthorne studies (which Mayo summarized in *Management and the Worker* in 1933),[1] concluded that "a factory performs two major functions: the economic one of producing goods and the social one of creating and distributing human satisfactions among the people under its roof."

The Hawthorne studies created a new field of investigation, industrial psychology, but they had an impact reaching far beyond that. They influenced the whole developing area of social psychology (one of Mayo's researchers was W. Lloyd Warner, who went on to help found the "Chicago school" of sociology, with its concepts of social-psychological stratification of the American community into "upper-upper, lower-upper, upper-middle," etc. groups).[2]

Hundreds of other researchers hastened to follow up Hawthorne with studies elsewhere. A major deficiency in Taylor's scientific management theory had been exposed. The new movement was sometimes given the name "human relations," and was regarded at first as a counter-movement to Taylorism. In reality the work of the industrial sociologist complemented that of the industrial engineer; by stressing the sociopsychological parameters of mass-production jobs, the behavioral scientist added new dimensions to the industrial engineer's concern with the worker's performance. With the realization that the worker had motivations beyond economic gain and humane physical treatment, scientific management took a long stride in the direction of becoming truly scientific.

Mayo's studies had suggested that consultation in the form of interviews between workers and management helped give workers a sense of being part of a team and thereby enlisted their cooperation. This proved a fruitful path for the future. In Mayo's words, "The belief of the individual in his social function and solidarity with a group—his capacity for collaboration in work" needed to be salvaged. L. Coch and J. R. P. French, Jr., carried out experiments, for example, that showed how groups permitted to participate in planning changes of work showed less resistance to the changes, achieved higher levels of output more quickly after the change, and displayed less dissatisfaction than non-participating groups.[3] The University of Michigan's Survey Research Center studied railway work gangs and groups of office workers and found that among both, high output was associated with employee-centered supervisors.[4] In Britain the Tavistock Institute of Human Relations reported on studies of British coal miners and on cotton textile workers in India, which showed that different forms of work organization within the same technology can lead to very different consequences. Their analysis employed the concept of a "socio-technical system," which comprehended both the technology and the work organization.[5] However, though many researchers in the 1930's and 1940's followed the path Mayo had blazed, and though industrial engineers sought to make use of the new findings, the large-scale application of "Mayoism" awaited a later date.

Meantime further studies in the conventional field with which the Hawthorne experiment had begun, the physical conditions affecting the worker, and especially the man-machine interface, yielded fresh results that were ultimately incorporated into a new professional discipline, "human engineering," or "human-factors engineering." Human-factors engineers do not seek to engineer humans, but seek to design machines to fit human physiological characteristics. Machinery and equipment are made to meet the parameters of the operator's strength, convenient reach, and normal timing. The shape of a shovel or a lever, the angle of a saw handle or foot pedal, the height of a lathe feed, and thousands of other tool and machine design considerations can be optimized by human factors engineering.[6] Frederick Winslow Taylor's famous "shovel science" was actually a pioneer example of human-factors engineering, which may be seen as a modern branch of Taylorism.

As factory production has grown more sophisticated,

many other considerations have arisen, for example, the design of control panels so that important dials are kept within peripheral vision of the monitor. The growth of complex control systems in automated factories is, in fact, the outstanding development in modern industrial production.

18. Sophistication of Production: The Logic of Automation

In 1946 D. S. Harder, executive vice-president of the Ford Motor Company, was studying plans for a new Ford engine plant to be built in Cleveland and a stamping plant to be built in Buffalo. He told his subordinates he wanted "more materials-handling equipment between these transfer machines. Give us some more of that automatic business . . . that 'automation.' " The word neatly summarized the new trend toward in-plant carriers that could not only move a casting from one machine to the next but could orient it with precision and feed it to the second machine. It caught on at once and soon was part of, first, the American and then the world's language (often rather loosely used).

Nevertheless, neither the idea nor the technology represented by "automation" was new in 1946.[1] Powered machinery capable of doing precision work, materials-handling equipment, and control systems, the three basic elements of the new technology, all had existed for decades. The transfer machine, a combination of powered machinery and materials-handling equipment, made its first definitely identified appearance in 1888, in the plant of the Waltham Watch Company of Waltham, Massachusetts. This machine fed parts successively to different lathes mounted on the same base. By the 1920's Morris Motors in Great Britain and Graham-Paige in the U.S. were moving automobile engine blocks through giant transfer machines with fifty or more electrically powered work stations. By 1946 transfer machines were widely employed not only in the automotive industry but in appliance manufacturing, electrical parts production, and many other metalworking industries. Without any human intervention, the work pieces were moved from one machining operation to the next, and accurately aligned for operation. The transfer machine obviously cut labor costs, and less obviously improved quality by insuring uniformity.

Automatic controls have an even longer pedigree than transfer machines.[2] The cam, a basic mechanical component known to the ancients and first used in machinery in the Middle Ages, is a classic illustration of automatic control. Typically in the form of an elliptical wheel that rotates to supply a reciprocal or other motion, the cam automatically adjusts the position of a lever or other machine element. During the nineteenth century cam controls were applied to many machine tools to make their actions automatic.

Cam controls have severe limitations, however, in respect to degree of movement, number of changes, speed, size, and sensitivity. Full automatic control cannot be attained unless the machine is sensitive to variations and adjusts itself to variable conditions. The process by which such response is achieved is known as feedback.

Examples of feedback controls can be found in earlier history. Thermostatic ovens, in which the fuel feed was governed by the oven's temperature, were developed by the seventeenth century. Denis Papin designed a safety valve for a steam engine in the seventeenth century, and in the eighteenth James Watt produced a classic example of mechanical feedback control in the flyball governor he invented for his steam engine. The flyball governor, already in use in grain mills, had weighted arms that swung farther away from a rotating vertical shaft as speed increased. Its function was to alter the gap between the two millstones to match changes in speed of the shaft. Watt made a fundamental change in the governor's action, using it to open and close a throttle valve and thereby regulate the engine's speed. The governor received information about the engine's speed from the rotating shaft, and acted on it, thus embodying the feedback principle that converts a merely automatic machine into a self-regulating machine. Another ingenious application of feedback was made by Watt's fellow Scotsman Andrew Meikle, who invented the fantail gear for windmills; a small windmill, set at right angles to the main windmill sails, that rotated a turret to keep the main sails facing into the wind.

Another significant line of development leading toward automation was that worked out by a succession of French inventors of the eighteenth century.

Seeking a method of programming textile looms for automatic production of a given pattern of weave, Basile Bouchon invented an automatic needle selector that was guided by a sheet of perforated paper. Jacques de Vaucanson improved the device in a model that Joseph-Marie

Jacquard discovered some years later, in need of repair, at the Paris Conservatory of Arts and Crafts. Jacquard perfected the device into a practical draw loom, automatically programmed by cards whose perforations controlled the loom's needles through a series of "yes-no" directions.

Jacquard's punched paper was later applied in the form of paper tape to the player piano and by 1897 to the monotype typesetting machine. Herman Hollerith used punched cards to tabulate U.S. census information in the 1890's, and finally a U.S. Air Force research project pioneered the tape control of machine processes, which became widespread in the 1950's. The process is known as "numerical control" because a numerical system, expressed magnetically or as punched holes, directs successive positions of tools, speeds, and feed rates on machine tools. The tape may contain a long series of instructions for the machine, controlling its performance of an entire succession of operations.

This and other lines of development converged in the electronic computer.[3] A remote ancestor of the computer was the ancient abacus, or calculating board, in which the technique of using place or position of physical objects —pebbles or beads—to indicate mathematical quantities was employed. John Napier of Scotland, the inventor of logarithms, built on the abacus principle with his famous "Napier's bones" or "Napier's rods" of the seventeenth century. These provided a mechanical multiplication table; by laying the proper rods side by side, each bearing the appropriate column of numbers, a table of multiples could be constructed mechanically. Using Napier's logarithmic principles, Edmund Gunter created the slide rule. In the same century, Blaise Pascal, the French mathematician-philosopher, invented the first mechanical adding

machine, followed a generation later by the first multiply-
ing machine, the creation of Gottfried Wilhelm Leibniz, the
co-inventor with Isaac Newton of calculus. Mechanical cal-
culators were refined and improved by a succession of later
inventors. Most notable of these was Charles Babbage, an
English genius of the nineteenth century whose "Analytical
Engine" represented an extraordinarily brilliant and
thoroughly worked-out conception that almost amounted
to the first information-processing computer. Unfortunately, Babbage's machine was never completed, and was so
far ahead of its time that it became completely forgotten
until the 1930's, when Howard Aiken, an American
mathematician-physicist, rediscovered Babbage's work
after spending three years going over the same ground.
Babbage had been handicapped by having only mechanical
components to use in his machine; Aiken had elec-
tromechanical elements which he assembled in 1944 into
the first operative computer. Aiken's "Harvard Mark I" was
succeeded only two years later by "ENIAC," an all-
electronic computer built at the University of Pennsylvania
by J. Presper Eckert and John W. Mauchly for the U.S.
Army. This proved to be the real wave of the future, especially when fortified by the demonstration by John von
Neumann that instructions could be encoded for such a
machine in the same language as the data the machine was
expected to use, so that data and instructions could be
coherently intermixed. With this principle, computers took
on a highly significant promise for industrial as well as
many other applications. Acting as a programming
machine and feedback-control system, a computer may
direct a single machine or a total production apparatus.

By 1958, the first computer-control applications were
operating in electric power generating plants and oil re-

fineries, to monitor performance and log data. Computer control was applied to the Port Arthur refinery of the Texas Oil Company in 1959, and the first computer-controlled chemical plant was opened by Imperial Chemical Industries of Great Britain the same year.

The fully automated industrial system comprises four elements: power source, sensing and feedback systems, programming elements, and decision-making devices. In its most complete form it has proved more adaptable to some industries than to others, and more applicable to flow processes than to batch processes. The chemical industry is an outstanding example, because of the ease with which gases and liquids can be moved between processing stations and the ease with which various measurements can be made. In some chemical plants a computer scans up to 2,000 characteristics such as pressure, temperature, flow rate, viscosity, and composition. If a programmed range is exceeded in one of these, the computer activates a light or sound signal.

Automation is by no means so complete in other industries. Although it entered the metallurgy field at an early date, and numerically controlled machine tools now produce large and complex pieces, there are still problems with preparing efficient control tapes, despite the development of computer languages. The automated assembly line is still in a primitive state, owing to the difficulty of designing transfer machines sensitive enough to give satisfactory positioning of workpieces for bolting and other fastening. Thus in the automotive industry, though complete engine production from a rough cylinder-block casting to a finished engine, including bearings and studs, has long been fully automated, the final assembly of an automobile must be done by men working in much the way that Henry Ford first organized them.

Despite difficulties, the impact of automation on production was substantial.[4] In the U.S. chemical industry, for example, the five-year period 1955-60 saw a decline of 3 percent in the number of workers while production expanded 27 percent. During the same period steel capacity increased 20 percent while the number of workers in the industry declined by 17,000, and in the U.S. meat industry 28,000 jobs were eliminated while production increased.

Even in industries where automation could for the time being be only partial, and when a large labor force was still required, the impact of automation on production efficiency was extraordinary. Japanese shipyards supply a striking example with their rapid construction of supertankers of several hundred thousand tons. At the Nippon Kokan Shipyard at Tsu, steel plates are fed into a computer-controlled process in which they are marked, cut, shaped, and welded into major hull blocks. These huge assemblies are then lifted by cranes straddling the building dock and welded into a hull by a largely automatic process. The T-shaped shipyard layout permits ships to be floated out for finishing at two points. In the Tsu yard, labor cost runs to only 20 percent, compared with 30 percent or more in U.S. and European yards.

Besides Japan and western Europe, Soviet Russia actively pursued a policy of maximum automation, an indication of which was the rapid increase in the number of workers classified by the Soviets as "mental" rather than "physical." At the start of Soviet industrialization in 1926 fewer than three million were so classified; by 1967 the number exceeded 27 million. One of the results was the resurrection in the USSR of the industrial-sociology movement that had been started as a socialist version of Taylorism and abandoned for some forty years. The Soviet authorities now had to take note of the same effects of automation on industrial (and other) work that were being felt in the western countries.

These effects were considerable, varied, and often unexpected. In the most completely automated industries, there has been a significant change in the worker's role. In the chemical industry he now typically monitors a control console governing a completely integrated production system. It is important to note that the worker does not himself control volume of output or quality; his responsibility is limited to watching the gauges and lights, listening for the alarm bells, or reading the printout telling whether the production elements are functioning as programmed. The computer does the rest. The late Norbert Wiener dreamed of a completely automatic factory, with no human agents involved.[5] If such an ideal could be achieved, if the human labor force could be completely eliminated, a control of accuracy and quality at a level unattainable by human skill could be achieved. But such total automation has not yet proved possible.

Because of the cost of highly automated machinery and computers, and because a malfunction in one element of an integrated system may shut down the entire line, the responsibility of the few workers in such a plant becomes exceptionally great. Automation may here be seen as a culmination of the centuries-old trends of increasing mechanization and of building skill into the machine, with the result of steadily decreasing the demand for human skill while steadily increasing the value of human judgment and responsibility.[6]

In the automated plant, the tool is no longer in any sense an adjunct of the worker's skill. Neither is the worker any longer an extension of the machine, as he appeared to become in assembly line production. The machine is now autonomous, performing its task in accordance with preplanned programming guided by the computer. To adapt the metaphor once used to describe the assembly line, in which the machine was pictured as the master and the worker as the slave, in the automated factory the machine appears to be the slave and the worker not the master but the overseer.

Besides altering the man-machine interface, the highly automated plant brings about an entirely new kind of problem in the organization of work: the machine-machine interface. This has two aspects, coordination between the controlling computer and the operating elements, and coordination between operating elements where transfer takes place from one to another. Engineers have had to develop new principles and techniques appropriate to this new machine-machine interplay.

The introduction of computers has also profoundly affected the organization of work in the information sector of the production economy.[7] In a manner analogous to the replacement of skilled mechanics by semi-skilled operators, clerks and bookkeepers are replaced by keypunch and tabulating-machine operators. Office work is undergoing the same mechanizaton as production; indeed, the information flow in offices has been likened to the flow of materials in manufacturing. Information, like materials, must be stored for retrieval. Typing or keypunching changes the form of the information just as a machine operation changes the form of the workpiece, and the value of the finished product is (presumably) enhanced by the addition of information to it. Finally, quality control is necessary to insure that the information is clear and accurate. Just as in the shop, the new automated machinery in the office has eliminated many information-processing jobs, such as monthly billing for purchases. In industrial production, clerical automation is invaluable for control of inventories of raw materials, parts, and finished goods.

The nature of the work in the automated industries, where heavy manual labor has been eliminated, has also had the effect of introducing women workers, contributing to a trend that by the 1970's made over one-third of the U.S. work force female.

Automation has also invaded many nonindustrial fields. In transportation it has appeared in the form of automatic ticket-reservation systems, automatic aircraft pilots, and automated flight trainers. Automatic takeoff and landing systems and automatic air-traffic control may be in the near future. Ground transportation has been slower to adopt automatic procedures, but a system of automatic freight car track-keeping for North America is under development. The new BART system of transportation in the San Francisco Bay area represents an ambitious pioneering effort. Japanese National Railways and others have introduced a substantial degree of automatic control in their newest train operations.

Considerable experimentation with automatic highway systems has not yet led to an economically viable system, though conventional traffic controls are increasingly automated. Banks, retail trade, medical facilities, libraries, and other institutions and economic areas are making increasing, sometimes spectacular, use of automation. An important recent development is the automated design system, in which a designer sketches details with a "light pen" on the face of a cathode-ray tube; the machine converts these into precise lines, and then via a computer translates them into instructions for a drafting machine or machine tool. In the design of electronic circuits, the system can be programmed to accept a statement of the function desired and to select the required components and their interconnecting paths.

All these developments suggest the enormous role that automation is destined to play in the immediate and more distant future.[8] It has already had an immense impact on economy and society in the U.S. and other advanced nations, although not in the sense once anticipated and feared.[9]

19. Acceleration of Change: The Impact of Automation

The automatic factory and assembly line without human agents are only so far ahead of us as is limited by our willingness to put such a degree of effort into their engineering as was spent, for example, in the development of the technique of radar in the Second World War.... There is no rate of pay [now] at which a pick-and-shovel laborer can live which is low enough to compete with the work of a steam-shovel as an excavator. The modern industrial revolution is similarly bound to devalue the human brain, at least in its simpler and more routine decisions. . . . [In] the second revolution . . . the average human being of mediocre attainments or less has nothing to sell that is worth anyone's money to buy.

—NORBERT WIENER[1]

Only two years after Harder had coined the word "automation" Dr. Norbert Wiener of Massachusetts Institute of Technology introduced another term, "cybernetics," which he used as the title of a book describing the potential widespread application of computers to production and distribution.

Within a few years, Wiener predicted, the "automatic age" would arrive, producing mass unemployment in U.S. industry. Wiener's pessimistic vision was immediately accepted by a large number of observers, and his fears even exaggerated. In 1963 a business reporter for a news magazine wrote a book predicting that automation would eliminate a million and a half jobs a year in America. The same year George Meany, president of the AFL-CIO, offered a figure of from 400,000 to 4,000,000 jobs lost a year, and forecast the ultimate production of all the goods needed by American society by one-quarter the existing work force. John I. Snyder, president of a firm manufacturing automation equipment, predicted that "upwards of 40,000 jobs a week" would be wiped out.

Three years later a more sober note was sounded by the National Commission on Technology, Automation, and Economic Progress appointed by President Lyndon B. Johnson. Despite some reluctance on the part of the group's labor members, the commission reported that the persistent (though not high) unemployment of the 1954-65 period was not the result of increasing mechanization and automation, but of demographic changes, government fiscal policies, and purely economic forces. The commission predicted that technological advances would eliminate jobs but not work, and that the government could always apply fiscal policies to spur economic growth and counter any threat to employment.

Subsequent experience has confirmed the commission's view. The spread of automation throughout industry has been considerably slower than Wiener anticipated, and its effect has been much more complex than he foresaw. A fascinating statistic is the estimate that no fewer than 50 million manual operators would be needed to handle today's traffic volume in the U.S. telephone system if no automation had been introduced. Obviously, 50 million telephone operators have not been laid off. The number of telephone employees has in fact increased, but not the number of operators. The real effect of automation in the telephone system has been to increase enormously the amount of telephone communication possible in the U.S.—and undoubtedly to contribute actually to bringing about such an increase. This effect, certainly widespread in other industries, is very similar to that of the earlier industrial revolution, where mechanization brought not unemployment but increased consumption.

The advance of automation is also related to an increasing international division of labor in which certain countries tend to specialize in certain types of industrial production, e.g., Japan in electronic consumer goods and the United States in computers.

In many countries, chronically short of labor, the threat of automation-created unemployment has proved scarcely more than a phantom. The Moscow News, answering a query from a reader in Gambia on effects of automation in the Soviet Union, cited "automation at the engineering enterprises of Kharkov" that made it possible "to free about 5,000 workers. . . . This was very important for the city's industry, which needed altogether 30,000 more workers than it had, so that those freed at the automated enterprises were a very welcome addition."[2] The lesson seems clear enough. It may be easier in the Soviet economy, which is not only planned, but which by comparison is still developing, to find industrial and other projects that need labor, but even superaffluent America has a sufficiency of need in many areas. The problem is not one of preserving existing jobs, but of redeploying the labor force.

A major direction of deployment was evident in U.S. census statistics that by 1960 showed the number of workers engaged in service industries exceeding the number in manufacturing. The "service industries" include virtually everyone not employed in direct production—government employees, salespeople, maintenance personnel—most of the white collars and some of the blue. Their numbers have grown not merely because modern society demands more services than formerly, but because the volume of consumer goods has risen so rapidly without a corresponding increase in the number of production workers, in other words because of the increase in mechanization and automation in production. We turn out more TV sets with fewer production workers, and as we do we create a need for more salesmen, repairmen, actors, technicians, advertising copywriters, and all the rest. This trend, marked in the U.S., is apparent also in western Europe, Japan, and even less advanced countries.

By the 1970's the specter of mass unemployment brought on by automation seemed relegated to the realm of mythology alongside the fears of the nineteenth-century machine wreckers.

Nevertheless, where automation was introduced, it changed the kind of work men did, and the education and skill required to do it. It increased the relative number of engineers, maintenance men, office employees, and others indirectly connected with the production process in relation to the number of production workers. Automated production jobs were reduced essentially to three types: machine monitoring or supervision, machine maintenance, and a very reduced number of unskilled workers for cleanup and other tasks. Although the maintenance men require a high degree of skill in mechanical, electronic, and hydraulic aptitudes, the prediction that the automated factory would place a premium on education has not been fulfilled. The degree of education required to monitor a control panel or to perform key-punch operations is not great. Some simple programming sometimes requires only a high school education and computer training. The pressure for higher educational backgrounds for workers in modern industry apparently comes less from the demands of the jobs themselves than simply from the ideology of employers and the psychology of employees who have been indoctrinated to equate education with income.

Perhaps paradoxically, automation often brings a reduction in the need for education. Just as a skilled machinist may be replaced by a numerically controlled machine monitored by a merely semi-skilled operator, so middle management may be replaced by computers operated by modestly skilled personnel. The design of certain types of equipment, such as electric motors and transformers, was traditionally done by an engineer who combined the specifications of the customer with the information in the standard manuals in accordance with procedures learned in college. But the engineer can now be replaced by a properly programmed computer and a modestly skilled operator.

Of all the effects of automation on the work force, the largest has undoubtedly been the shift in its composition from blue collar to white collar. More and more of the knowledge and skill content of the production process is being transferred from the machine operator to the computer and its white-collar attendants.

Within the plant, in the period before World War II, the job foreman usually set the production schedule for his department. Now, increasingly, the job foreman is presented with a detailed production schedule by a young engineer in the front office. Maintenance men formerly set their own procedures for servicing machines; now the maintenance procedure is detailed by the plant engineer.

Peter Drucker has pointed out that the increasing concentration of "knowledge jobs" has had its major impact in uprooting the traditions of skilled craftswork.[3] Our industrial organization has presupposed that carpenters, electricians, and other craftsmen possessed differentiated skills. Now the tendency is to regard craft skills as being much alike, the carpenter's little different from the electrician's. Skilled jobs now require skill elements from several previously separate crafts. Where work on the steam engine was performed by boiler makers, sheet metal workers, and electricians, on a modern diesel engine work is organized not by craft specialties but by stages in the process: undercarriage, motor assembly, final assembly. As Edward Ames and Nathan Rosenberg have observed,[4] the more specialized a man, the fewer tasks he can perform. Skilled workers who perform many tasks are relatively unspecialized, while machine operators who perform only one are highly specialized. The same is true of machinery. Ames and Rosenberg point out that the increased division of labor of the twentieth century has taken the form of introducing less specialized machinery (machines that do several tasks instead of only one) and thus permitting one specialized worker, the machine operator, to perform as many tasks as several workers using specialized machines did in the past.

All the above backgrounds a new paradox in the blue-collar, white-collar situation. While the blue-collar worker is less and less chained to a specific production task, the white-collar worker seems to be moving toward a narrower and narrower range of functions.

As for the effects of automation on the life and work conditions of men and women, it can scarcely be disputed that overall they have been beneficial. The primary result of automation has been exactly the same as that of every other major advance in production technology, to increase per capita output while lessening human drudgery. Better pay, shorter hours, better sanitation and safety conditions, and paid vacations have accrued. In the United States the factory workweek shrank from 65.7 hours in 1850 to 38 in 1960. This overall improvement of the life situation of the worker has by no means been confined to fully automated or partly automated or even highly mechanized plants; it has spread throughout all industry. A very noteworthy feature of mass production in the advanced countries in modern times has been the tendency for wages, hours, and working conditions to achieve a near uniform pattern through a whole national economy. One explanation of this phenomenon is the new mobility of the worker who, if he is dissatisfied with pay in one industry, can transport himself and his family to another region, another industry. This mobility of labor has been marked in both Europe and the United States.

The trend toward wage standardization has been vertical as well as horizontal, in many cases virtually eliminating pay differentials in mass-production industry.[5] In the U.S. Steel Corporation, some 5,000 job classifications involve only minor or no wage differentials. A man advanced from coal handler second class to coal handler first class receives virtually no pay increment, with the implication that the psychological satisfaction of the higher classification is of sufficient value.

Against the advantages of the new production techniques must be set the disadvantages. Some of the new leisure time is lost to the demands of transportation as workers live farther and farther from their jobs. One study, by Sebastian de Grazia for the Twentieth Century Fund, indicated that today's U.S. factory worker has only slightly more net free time than his nineteenth-century predecessor.[6] Some of the value of increased pay is inevitably lost to inflation, which, contrary to some beliefs, victimizes wage workers more than middle-class people who own real estate and stocks. It must also be emphasized that many of the old-fashioned factory problems still remain in all countries—dirty, noisy plants, unsafe, and unhealthy working conditions, physically exhausting labor.

A serious and growing problem in all the advanced countries is that of transferring workers from one industry to another. As the pace of first industrialization and then of mechanization and automation increases, more and more occupations are made obsolete, either by reason of the substitution of machines for men or by the elimination of the need for the industry itself. The effects are felt by the white-collar worker as well as by the blue, and the most highly educated segment of the work force is not immune.

Increasing mechanization places a larger and larger premium not on any particular skill, or even on skill itself, but on adaptability. That workers are more adaptable than was once thought has been demonstrated in many countries in the twentieth century, especially in the two World Wars, when European and American men and women made radical changes in occupations under great pressures and within short time spans. Yet the special conditions and atmosphere of war production may not provide a very satisfactory guide for peacetime industrial change.

The psychological difficulties of adjusting men and women of all skill categories to sudden terminations, not merely of jobs, but of occupations, with the need to learn entirely new, perhaps unrelated skills, are surely formidable. A radical change has taken place since Dr. James B. Conant in *Slums and Suburbs* in 1961 deplored the decline of vocational education. The *Work in America* study, published in 1972 by the U.S. Department of Health, Education and Welfare, condemned vocational education on the high school level as "unrealistic" and "very expensive" because it trains young workers in skills that may soon be outmoded. Charles Silberman in his provocative book *The Crisis in the Classroom* (1970) made the charge more broadly: "Nothing could be more widely impractical than an education designed to prepare [today's children] for specific vocations or professions or facilitate their adjustment to the world as it is. To be practical, an education should prepare [them] for work that doesn't yet exist and whose nature cannot even be imagined."

Charles DeCarlo, former Director of Education for IBM and later president of Sarah Lawrence College, has also stressed the importance of broad rather than specialized education for today's job world, which he characterizes as above all "an idea world."[7]

Here clearly lies a major challenge for the last quarter of the century. It is a challenge that at least has the advantage of being fairly definable: a lifelong educational system is needed to provide the additional training (vocational and other) that people need to cope with a changing technological society.

But in terms of immediate impact on today's workers, the most significant impact of modern production techniques consists of two largely intangible elements: tension and boredom.

The old-time craftsman, whatever the problems of his life, was little afflicted by tension deriving from the work he did. It might demand an exceptionally high degree of skill and concentration, but for that very reason it was interesting and rewarding. The goldbeater who slowly worked a piece of precious metal with thousands of accurately aimed, delicately delivered blows of his small hammer, the last passage of which effaced the marks of the hammer, loved his work. Not so the worker on Henry Ford's assembly line whose degree of job satisfaction, according to Ford, depended on the degree to which he did not have to pay attention to what he was doing.

The *Work in America* study cited a case where a factory worker deliberately "knocked a dent" in the product he was making "to do something to make it really unique."

Today's automobile assembly line workers, even though their physical labor has been reduced by materials-handling machinery, suffer from the noise, monotony, and tension of their job exactly as did their predecessors. Harvey Swados' keenly observed *On the Line* of 1957 and Arthur Hailey's *Wheels* of 1971 show very similar pictures:

His surroundings meant nothing to Walter, who had not expected the factory to look like an art gallery. But the work, and the conditions under which he had to do it, were a nightmare of endless horror from which Walter sometimes thought, stumbling wearily out of the plant after ten hours of unremitting anguish, he would one day awaken with a scream. It was not simply that the idea of working on an endless succession of auto bodies as they came slowly but ineluctably rolling down the assembly line like so many faceless steel robots was both monotonous and stupefying, or that the heavy work of finding bumps and dents in them, knocking them out and filing them down, was in itself too exhausting. No, it was the strain of having to work both fast and accurately, with the foreman standing over him and glaring through his thick-lensed glasses, that made Walter dread the beginning of each day. . . .

—*On the Line*

He was learning: first, the pace of the line was faster than it seemed; second, even more compelling than the speed was its relentlessness. The line came on, and on, and on, unceasing, unyielding, impervious to human weakness or appeal. It was like a tide which nothing stopped except a half-hour lunch break, the end of a shift, or sabotage.

—*Wheels*

The fiction writers' picture has been very adequately corroborated in interviews with auto workers, one of whom added this fillip: "Sometimes the line breaks down. When it does we all yell 'Whoopee!' "[8]

A significant study of automobile workers in 1965 showed that the assembly line worker, despite improvements in his material situation brought about through his union, tended to regard both his job and himself with contempt.

Workers in more automated industries experience less boredom but perhaps more tension. Even though the job of monitoring a control panel demands relatively little skill, it requires constant alertness with high penalties for failure. Carelessness can not only destroy a large production run but may damage expensive capital equipment. One study that focused on the overall satisfaction of three kinds of workers—craftsmen, workers in mechanized industries, and workers in automated industries—produced statistics showing a wide variation. The craftsmen predictably scored highest, with 87 percent expressing a high degree of satisfaction. The automated-plant workers were next, with 52 percent, while the mechanized-plant workers scored only 14 percent.

The problem has attracted wide discussion in the 1960's and 1970's under the name of "worker alienation," or "blue-collar blues," or, in Emile Durkheim's word of eighty years ago, resurrected and still valid, or perhaps more valid than ever, "anomie." That collective bargaining today centers more and more on holidays, time off, and breaks in the working day is symptomatic. Very notable is the emphasis in the U.S. auto industry on "30-and-out," the slogan for retirement after thirty years on the assembly line. In the 1973 round of negotiations at Chrysler, the sticking point was management's right to impose overtime, especially on weekends. Despite high overtime pay, the workers wanted to have the option of taking the weekend break. "What good is the paycheck," the workers were asking, "if you don't have time to enjoy it?"

A more ominous signal is the appearance in Detroit of an organization called CHIP, an acronym for "Curb Heroin in Plants." A CHIP counselor succinctly summarized the root cause of widespread drug addiction in a huge gear-and-axle plant on Detroit's East Side: "The job belittles a man's intelligence."

The *Work in America* study reached these pessimistic conclusions:

> The discontent of trapped, dehumanized workers is creating low productivity, increasing absenteeism, high worker turnover rates, wildcat strikes, industrial sabotage, poor quality products and a reluctance by workers to give themselves to their tasks.
>
> Work-related problems are contributing to a decline in physical and mental health, decreased family stability and community cohesiveness, and less 'balanced' political attitudes.
>
> Growing unhappiness with work is also producing increased drug abuse, alcohol addiction, aggression and delinquency in the work place and in the society at large.

According to a study quoted in *Work in America*, the "potent factors that impinge on the worker's values" are "those that concern his self-respect, a chance to perform well in his work, a chance for personal achievement and growth in competence, and a chance to contribute something personal and unique to his work. . . . Those workers with jobs that measure high on variety, autonomy, and use of skills were found to be low on measures of political and personal alienation. . . .

> Knowledge, not skill, is the critical factor in modern technology. For example, craftsman who can square off a piece of steel with a hand file may be a true artisan; but his artisanship is useless on a numericaly controlled machine tool which needs someone who understands a system.

Noting that blue-collar workers are better educated than ever before while their jobs require little exercise of judgment, the study says that "we begin to see one of the real causes of their blues. These better educated workers . . . are not so easily satisfied as their forebears with the quality of most blue-collar jobs."

White-collar and management personnel are also affected. Form-filling and other routine paperwork, steadily increasing in offices and institutions, seldom provide job satisfaction. A British clerk wrote of himself in the third person, "Unlike even the humblest worker on a production line, he doesn't produce anything. He battles with phantoms, abstracts; runs in a paper chase that goes on year after year, and seems utterly pointless."[9]

Anomie, however, is not restricted to blue-collar and clerical groups. A survey conducted by the American Management Association revealed that a third of the top management group defined success in terms that had little or no relationship to their career jobs, while among middle and lower management personnel the figure was nearly two-thirds.[10] Two-thirds of this second group also expressed the significant opinion that the organizations they worked for were not interested in or even aware of their real aspirations. This finding echoes with extraordinary fidelity a kind of complaint often voiced by the blue collars.

An overwhelming percentage, better than four out of five, of the executives interviewed agreed that their attitudes to achievement and success were changing. Most felt that their basic life objectives were personal, private, and family-centered.

In many cases the executives' advantages over the plant workers in respect to dirt, noise, and physical labor, are balanced by longer hours and a higher exposure to tension.

Thus for many top executives the only advantage enjoyed over the lowest plant worker is a higher scale of pay and fringe benefits. That these are not always sufficient to compensate for the tension has been demonstrated by many executive "drop-outs" such as the Chicago banker who quit to run a vegetable stand and the West Coast telephone executive who switched to a low-paying job counseling the disadvantaged.

Thus, from the top to the bottom of the working hierarchy the modern corporate industrial production unit is populated with men and women whose deepest feelings about what they are doing with their working lives are frequently negative and unsatisfactory. A complete reversal has taken place. Where once workers enjoyed their work but were unable to produce enough to give themselves leisure and material satisfactions, now they are gaining the leisure and material satisfactions while losing the enjoyment of work.

20. Management's New Task: Beating the Blue-Collar Blues

The response of industrial management (and in fact of society in general) to the problems of alienation summarized in the previous chapter promises to be second only to increased automation and mechanization as a significant element in the organization of work in the 1970's and 1980's. Classic problems of worker discontent, it is now generally conceded, have been intensified by the larger scale of operations and by external forces created by increased production.

Changing technology, even while representing a continuation of past trends, is once more outdating the organization of work. Authority in the old-time factories was a hierarchical, pyramidal, military-type chain of command, with the head of the corporation or factory at the top and various levels of supervision fanning out below to the mass of workers at the base.[1] But today production workers no longer constitute so large a mass, and "knowledge" workers distort the pyramid shape. In addition, the development of communications and information devices has changed the tasks of middle and top management, just as new machinery has changed the job of the production worker.

Instead of a pyramid the diagram of the organization of work in industry resembles an outline of the human nervous system, or perhaps the circuit diagram of a computer. Complexes of production centers are interwoven and interrelated in a highly intricate pattern. To take fullest advantage of the machinery now employed in industry requires changes in work patterns and even attitudes.

In some continuous-process industries, such as chemicals, petroleum, steel, and glass, machinery works around the clock. This trend is growing in the effort to achieve high and efficient utilization of costly equipment. Any attempt by workers to limit production by machines has the reverse effect of encouraging the introduction of more machinery to substitute for an inefficient labor force, while the increased goods and leisure made available to the worker by improved production create new attitudes that in turn affect the worker's performance and entail further changes in the organization of work.

Most of the problems of the present and near future organization of work therefore center in motivation of the worker. Early nineteenth-century mill workers, unorganized and unprotected by law, were forced to work long and hard hours because the alternative was starvation. Very characteristically, the factory owners and foremen complained of the laziness and incompetence of their working force. Frederick Winslow Taylor made the first move toward motivating the mass-production worker by offering material incentives for increased productivity. Taylor's concept of "mechanical man" proved defective in its ignoring of human motivations beyond the material. At a certain point the workers refused to respond to the material incentives, and a battle developed between the industrial engineers and the workers who sought to outwit the time-study man and his stopwatch. "Scientific" standards for work did not synchronize well with natural human tendencies; the subdivision of the job into narrow, repetitive tasks failed to meet human psychological needs. As worker anomie set in, further subdivision of work became only marginally effective in increasing productivity and improving quality.

The Hawthorne experiments revealed that worker productivity was not exclusively related to physical environment and material rewards. In fact Elton Mayo and his associates showed that production could rise on the motivation of workers impelled by a mere illusion. What the workers wanted, the Hawthorne data showed, was a sense of someone taking a special interest in their performance.

After the Hawthorne study, problems of the organization of work ceased to be the exclusive province of economists and industrial engineers and became a field of study for new specialists in the behavioral sciences —industrial psychologists and industrial sociologists. This trend, begun in the 1920's, was accelerated with the increasing mechanization of industry following World War II, and was still growing in the 1970's. The future organization of work will undoubtedly be based more and more on investigations made by behavioral scientists and the application of their findings to the work patterns.

Once regarded as an art, production management is

increasingly given scientific treatment, both in the field and as an academic study. A major development in the initiation of this trend was the establishment of schools of "Business Administration" between the two World Wars. The Harvard Graduate School of Business Administration, one of the leaders, showed its scientific bias by focusing its curriculum on empirical business practice, utilizing case studies of real-life business problems to train future executives. Harvard and other schools have increasingly used the tools of science: quantification and mathematical modeling, now aided by the capabilities of the computer. In the 1970's the business schools were turning away from studies based on narrow economic or financial concerns toward a behavioral-science orientation through a newly emerging discipline terming itself "management science," which used such newly developed tools as operations research.

Changing technology—mechanization and automation—brought about change in the organization of work that dictated a new approach, scientific and holistic, to management. When machines began performing mechanical tasks previously done by workers, and the workers became monitors of the machines, the need for scientific analysis of work problems heightened to include communication within the factory organization and communication between man and machine.

At first, managerial tasks followed the trend in the division of labor in the factory, that is, they were broken down into small units or functions. This approach was found inappropriate, since responsibility, subdivided, was weakened. New types of organizational structure, *i.e.*, the "nervous system" as opposed to the pyramid model, and new assignments of authority and responsibility were devised. Just as the worker had to become adaptive to changing technology, so did management. Recent emphasis has been on "free-form" management, meaning the creation of specific organizational approaches to meet the needs of particular segments of a large, complex organization. New organizational concepts like "product management" and "project management" are employed, in which the responsibility for the development and marketing of a product or the carrying-through of a project is placed in the hands of an individual and his team, equipped with the resources needed to do the job.[2] This "systems approach" was pioneered by the Manhattan Project of World War II, the U.S. space effort of the 1960's, and other enterprises of great magnitude. The old hierarchical forms of organization had to be discarded because communications were inhibited by the number of intermediaries between the top decision-makers and those entrusted with transforming decisions into action. More recently computer technology has been enlisted to help solve communications problems in very large projects.

Meantime, the increasing mechanization of production in the 1970's once more stirred fears of mass unemployment. Unlike the apprehensions of the 1950's, when automation first reared its head, current trends do not point to structural unemployment, that caused by changes in the technological structure of industry. Rather the 1970's trend is toward maintaining the overall work force by shrinking the workweek while increasing the productivity of each worker. There is also a continuation of the steady shift of workers from manufacturing to service industries, the whole trend converging with the development of solutions to worker anomie.

Past experience has demonstrated that improvements in technology—both the machines and the organization of work—have constantly increased the productivity of the individual worker. Thus movements to reduce the workweek, to lengthen vacations, to provide for earlier retirement, and to delay entrance into the work force, are built on the assumption that the worker will be able to produce as much or more through the course of his working life despite putting in many fewer hours. There are indications that the loss in working time is actually less than it appears on paper—shorter workweeks reduce absenteeism, while the elimination of older workers from the work force improves average performances.

Of the productivity gains made by American workers in the past through increased mechanization and changes in the organization of work, two-thirds have been in real wages and one-third in increased leisure. Many labor unions in the 1970's favored a 32-hour week in four eight-hour days. Perhaps an intermediate step toward this goal is the redistribution of the existing 36-to-40-hour workweek into four ten-hour days. Adopted or tried in many places, the change has often brought gains in productivity. The longer days sometimes result in greater fatigue, reducing efficiency, but many companies found that an increase in efficiency occurred instead, due to higher worker morale. A notable effect was that absenteeism was radically reduced. One company went the next step further, combining the four-day week with a 10 percent reduction in hours. It reported a 75 percent drop in absenteeism with a net production gain of 6 percent.

An experiment in 1973 in a textile mill in Georgia put 100 knitting employees on a three-day, 36-hour week and also gave them six weeks' vacation. Productivity improved markedly, and absenteeism in the experimental division dropped to a third of the company-wide rate.

An even more radical departure from traditional hours of work has been tried out with success in European industry. Some 3,500 West German firms, for example, have adopted "sliding time" schedules, in which the doors of the factory are open 12 hours (sometimes more, sometimes less) a day, while factory and office workers come to work and quit when they please, provided only that they put in a 40-hour week, and that they are present for a "core period" in the middle of the day. The few American companies that have tried "flexitime" have concurred in the European report that the plan cuts losses due to absenteeism, tardiness, unrecorded leave, and even sick leave, since workers have time to take care of personal affairs that formerly inspired "monthly flu."[3]

The theory of "flexitime" is perhaps put into perspective by an incident related in *Work in America*. A night foreman checking on three young janitors in an office building found all three sitting in an office, one reading a newspaper, a second asleep, and the third studying. The foreman exploded and gave the men a written warning, which they promptly protested to their union. "We cleaned all those offices in five hours instead of eight," they argued. "What more do they want?" The union steward's "solution" was to talk the young men into "stretching out" their work to cover eight hours. "Now everyone's happy," he reported. He was surely wrong—management and union might be happy, but the young janitors must have been left angry and frustrated.

Certainly more imaginative was the classic (1932) British motivational study of girl workers threading embroidery needles, a repetitive task since taken over by automatic machinery. The girls were told first that they had to thread a hundred dozen needles a day instead of the seventy-five dozen they had been threading. The announcement produced consternation that turned to delight when it was added that on finishing the hundred dozen they could go home. They got through the new quota in time to leave at 2:30 in the afternoon.[4]

One of the most attractive formulas for reducing anomie in the 1970's appeared to be "job enrichment."[5] An early approach was simply to rotate jobs, alternating workers among two or more tasks over periods of a few weeks. A more sophisticated method is to improve the worker's satisfaction with his job by giving greater scope for personal achievement and recognition, making the job more challenging, and allowing the worker opportunity for individual advancement and growth.

Instead of rationalizing the work task to increase efficiency, as Taylor and the scientific-management experts tried to do, job enrichment attempts to motivate workers by providing psychological satisfaction. Where the industrial engineer sought to structure the physical job for optimum efficiency, and the organizational theorist focused on the personnel hierarchy of the factory, the behavioral scientist concerns himself with job attitudes. He admits the importance of physical setup and factory organization in workers' attitudes, but he seeks to go beyond them.

Frederick Herzberg, a prominent industrial psychologist, has identified five factors as strong determinants of job satisfaction—achievement, recognition, work itself, responsibility, and advancement—and has formulated a "motivation-hygiene theory" designed to re-educate both management and workers to these "motivators" which would make for both greater human satisfaction and a more humane utilization of manpower.[6]

Not every job in every production process yields enrichment potential. Nevertheless, enrichment is believed to promise substantial gains not only in terms of human satisfaction but in material profit across a broad spectrum of industry, reducing job turnover, absenteeism, errors, strikes, and other damaging factors.[7]

By the 1970's job enrichment had been tried out in a number of companies both in the U.S. and abroad. The Bell Telephone Company at first called its application "Work Itself," later "Job Restructuring," and defined the purpose as giving the employee more responsibility according to the individual's ability and willingness to take on such responsibility.[8] The motivation theory on which the Bell company operates postulates that the causes of job satisfaction and job dissatisfaction are not simple opposites, and that the main sense of satisfaction comes from the nature of the work. A man who dislikes stamping metal, according to this theory, may also resent the fact that he gets only two weeks' vacation, but doubling his vacation to four weeks will not decrease by half his aversion to stamping metal. To get at that it is necessary to change the way he does the job or to move him to another job.

Putting the theory into practice did not prove easy at Bell. Seven years after the "Work Itself" experiments demonstrated the value of the concept, and despite support from top-level management, less than a quarter of Bell System managers were found making practical application of the techniques they had been given. "Making changes is always inconvenient, especially toward the unknown," said Dr. Robert N. Ford, Bell Director of Work Organization and Environmental Research. "Some managers just can't seem to let go. They're afraid to give up precise controls, afraid to depend on employees to perform their work. We know job enrichment techniques will work if they're given the chance. Now we've got to find the key to motivating middle and upper-level managers to try these job-enrichment concepts."

Another Bell executive pointed out a subtle element in the psychology of job enrichment: "[Managers] have been ingrained with a philosophy that says in order to treat people fairly, you have to treat them all the same way."

Yet where applied, job enrichment at Bell has had a high degree of success in combating one of the company's biggest problems—high job turnover. At Indiana Bell, phone directories were formerly compiled by women employees each of whom performed only one of the 17 operations necessary in compiling a directory. The ghosts of Adam Smith, Josiah Wedgwood, Henry Ford, and Frederick Taylor all may have applauded the minute division of labor, but Indiana Bell management found itself endlessly hiring and training new workers. Under the job enrichment ideology, each worker was given an entire directory to compile, performing all 17 steps, from scheduling to proofreading. Turnover dropped substantially.

A similar experience was reported from a company manufacturing hot plates. In good old-fashioned Smith-Taylor-Ford fragmentation of the work task, each woman employee had a single repetitive job to perform over and over. Management was dissatisfied not only with productivity but with quality control, because of a high rate of rejects. Procedure was changed; each girl was permitted to assemble the entire hot plate. The reject rate dropped from 23 percent to 1 percent, while productivity rose 47 percent and absenteeism declined from 8 percent to 1 percent.

A significant aspect of the "Worker Alienation Bill" introduced by Senator Edward M. Kennedy in 1973 was its emphasis on "training and retraining professionals and subprofessionals in work humanization approaches and methods." Such training was felt to be critically important by most of the witnesses at the bill's hearings because of the impact that industrial engineers and plant designers have on the condition of work and their present lack of concern for the worker."

An outgrowth of the fifty-year-old Hawthorne studies is a trend toward worker participation in the organization of the job. Interesting experiments were under way in the 1970's in several countries. In 1971 the Volvo and Saab automobile factories in Sweden introduced a system of team production by which they in effect disassembled the assembly line. Auto and truck components, such as brake assemblies, were distributed to small groups of four to seven workers who decided themselves the order in which to perform the job, and who were given a voice in selecting their foremen. Favorable results were reported in improved morale and increased productivity.

Even earlier, Japanese industry began introducing what were called "worker circles," consisting of about a dozen men engaged in a common task who make their own decisions on production methods and quality control. Some 400,000 such teams now exist in Japanese plants. Productivity per man-hour in Japan has risen at a rapid rate through the 1960's and 1970's. The most important contributing element has doubtless been capital investment in machinery, but the strong loyalty inspired in Japanese workers by management policies is certainly worthy of note. James G. Abegglen has described in *Management and Worker: The Japanese Solution* (1973) how this loyalty is inspired by the paternalistic practices much used by Japanese corporate management.[9] In Japan the job involves much more than the "wage nexus" which Marx used to describe employer-employee relationships: It is a lifetime commitment on the part of both worker and management. Upon graduation from school, a Japanese takes a job where he is virtually guaranteed employment for life, with wage increases as he accumulates seniority and with little likelihood of being laid off in times of depression or being fired for incompetency (another job, suitable to his level of competency, is found for him within the firm). The company provides cheap meals at company dining rooms, low-cost medical care, dormitories for single workers and homes for married ones, company vacation resorts, raises and bonuses for marriage and children, and a social life—including athletic teams—centered in the company and one's fellow workers. It is understandable that the Japanese worker feels that he is a member of a family—a corporate family, to be sure, with the corporate managers playing the role of family elders. Under such circumstances, the "worker circles" are groupings within the family.

In a new plant built by Fiat in southern Italy in the early 1970's, four small assembly lines were installed instead of the conventional single large line, in order to let each worker remain with each car four minutes instead of one minute. A survey of Fiat worker attitudes revealed an interesting division: Older workers in general showed little enthusiasm and apparently did not care one way or the other, but younger workers favored the new arrangement.[10]

In West Germany, Israel, Norway, and Yugoslavia, government, business management, and labor leaders have collaborated in experiments aimed at increasing worker participation in decision-making. American plants have also experimented with the team approach. One textile mill set up teams of four and gave them complete responsibility for a group of machines, including operation, maintenance, and quality level. The groups are self-sustaining in that when a person leaves he is replaced by someone picked by the group itself.[11]

A dramatic example of worker participation in decision making came about through a threatened closing of a steel-pipe plant in California in 1973. Management at the Kaiser Steel plant in Fontana, faced with severe cost competition from Japanese steel makers, agreed to listen to some suggestions from the workers. Adjustments in plant equipment were made that reduced spoilage from 29 percent to 9 percent, and others that produced a steadier flow of production with fewer idle machines. Beyond these improvements management reported dividends from a "new spirit" in the plant that brought about swifter repair of machinery and better quality control. A union official summarized it: "Being recognized as people who can make creative suggestions has given the men a certain dignity." Because labor costs represent only a small fraction of the cost of making steel pipe, the improvement was less significant to the plant's competitive position than it might seem; nevertheless, in the context of the work-organization problems of the 1970's, the incident has undeniable significance.[12]

"Perhaps the most consistent complaint reported to our task force," said the *Work in America* study, "has been the failure of bosses to listen to workers who wish to propose better ways of doing their jobs."

Not all jobs can be enriched, and not all workers' complaints can be met by job enrichment. Low pay, insecurity, inadequate fringe benefits, poor working conditions, and inappropriate job assignments remain problems outside the potential of job enrichment to solve.

But the worldwide attempts to improve the man-machine, worker-manager, and worker-worker interfaces seem too clearly dictated by the imperative of technology to be mere fads. The machine, through its advance in complexity, continues to transform the organization of work, and in its present phase the direction of transformation is evidently away from the old nexus of impersonal relationships based solely or primarily on material incentives and toward a new kind based on the psychological needs of humans as well as the requirements of the machine.

David Riesman, author of *The Lonely Crowd*, has recently reconsidered his conclusion that efforts to improve the meaningfulness of work were futile, and that workers should instead be encouraged to seek meaning in leisure-time activities. "It might be easier to make leisure more meaningful," Riesman now believes, "if one at the same time could make work more demanding. . . . We cannot . . . make leisure more creative, individually and socially, if work is not creative, too."[13]

That we are moving toward ever greater worker participation in the industrial process can hardly be doubted. In the Chrysler negotiations mentioned earlier the settlement gave the workers the right to refuse to work overtime under certain conditions, something that would have been quite unthinkable a few years earlier. Modern industrial labor contracts have become extremely elaborate, and while they outline wage structures meticulously, they go into the most minute detail in connection with the rights of the worker —time for lunch, coffee breaks, even "goof-off" time. Perhaps most significant is the elaborate grievance structure set forth, embracing a hierarchy of officials, from shop stewards on up, to adjudicate complaints. In some industries grievance adjudication boards, composed of union and management representatives, sit throughout the year to insure settlement of all problems as they come up, rather than leaving the unsettled ones to contract negotiating time.

Union contracts in the U.S. and Europe have thus unmistakably qualified management's once total freedom to hire and fire. How far will this trend go? An augury of the new era in industrial relations may be found in a report by David Jenkins from the Grangesberg Company, a Swedish steel, mining, and shipping combine.[14] Inge Selinder, the personnel director for the huge company, told Jenkins: "The employer's right to fire people must be taken away. If someone doesn't fit the organization it means we recruited badly. And if we make a mistake we must take the consequences." Such deliberate no-firing policies are actually in effect today in many industrial plants, not only in Sweden but elsewhere, notably Japan. Henry Ford and Frederick Taylor would, to say the least, be astonished.

21. Over the Horizon: Fears and Hopes

The organization of work is the way in which men group themselves and their tools to produce the goods and services necessary to maintain life and society. It is affected by changes in society as a whole, and it in turn induces such changes. It fosters new technology and it is itself shaped by technological advance. Its progress and convolutions profoundly affect the life of all the individuals caught up in it, especially in Western society, where a man's role in the productive process largely determines his worth in the eyes of society.

Emile Durkheim asserted that "The ideal of human fraternity can be realized only in proportion to the progress in the division of labor, [which] . . . more and more tends to become the essential condition of social solidarity."[1] The interdependence of modern society, a mirror of the interdependence of modern production methods, certainly makes imperative a high degree of division of labor. Yet the newest trends in industrial relations seem to imply a reversal of Durkheim's dictum: "The ideal of human fraternity" is being called on to help prepare the new division of labor rather than to be the result. The concern for the worker's motivation and his participation in determining the conditions and even nature of his work may be seen as an element in the broad movement called "participatory democracy," the assumption by the individual citizen of a more direct role in a range of communal activities such as education and health care.

At least one authority, Daniel Bell, has begun turning needed attention to the embryonic "post-industrial" society,[2] one aspect of which can be seen in the shift from manufacturing to service industries. Along with personnel, technology is also making the shift to the service sector, notably in the computer system's assumption of paperwork tasks. How rapidly and how far this trend will go is difficult to estimate, but it seems clear enough that some of the problems of the recent past in the production section will be repeated. A decline in demand for unskilled labor and a shortage of trained technicians and professionals will place a premium on a flexible education system capable of giving an appropriately broad training to the young and assisting with programs for updating of skills throughout the worker's life. Ultimately, it is reasonable to anticipate a blending of production and service sectors as far as the work organization function is concerned, with both physical and mental drudgery taken over by the machine.

Despite all the complex problems and difficulties, the emerging pattern of organization of work promises to maintain its undeniably liberating effect on the masses of workers.

Robert Blauner, in *Alienation and Freedom*,[3] concludes

that "automation increases the worker's control over the work process and checks the further division of labor and growth of large factories." Many momentous new social trends have at least a discernible relationship to the changing industrial pattern. One of the most significant social trends in Europe, Japan, and the U.S. has been the rapidly changing status of women. As the machine abolished much onerous factory labor and created a demand for an army of clerical workers, the number of women in the labor force mounted. Household technology in the form of electrical appliances facilitated the movement of even wives and mothers into the work force on either a part-time or full-time basis. The 1970 U.S. Census showed 29.2 million women employees, many of whom may be said to have taken the place not of men, but of children, who are no longer entering the labor market at as early an age. Such changes in the organization of work as a reduction in the workday or the workweek also affect the man-woman relationship by giving the father of a family more time at home and a greater role in child-raising. The social and cultural impact in this sphere of the changing organization of work has already been great, and promises to be much greater. The age-old sexual division of labor appears headed for total extinction as physical strength ceases to be a factor in an automated, "unisex" work world.

The once widespread fear that invasion of the work arena by women would rob men of jobs (as it in fact did in the painful days of the original Industrial Revolution) has evidently been buried along with most of the apprehensions about automation. The number of workers, both men and women, in the work forces of all the advanced countries continues to increase as automation proceeds. Forecasts based on this trend seem certain to remain valid for the next few decades, with allowances for gradual reduction of working hours and working lifetimes. If there is any surprise ahead in this area it will probably be the relative suddenness with which reductions take place in working hours. Certainly it is some cause for wonder that hardly any significant reductions in work time in either factory or office have taken place since World War II, and we may well consider such reductions overdue.

Indeed, at the end of 1973 and beginning of 1974 there were predictions—and a few actual cases—of large-scale reductions in worktime (usually to a four-day workweek). But these were inspired by the shortage of energy (or the shortage of raw materials caused by the "energy crisis"), and were not in response to growing productivity through automation. Yet these reductions in worktime might prove to be lasting beyond any energy crisis, if industries are able to maintain previous production levels on a four-day schedule. Within a few years the worker's expression of release may well be "Thank God, it's Thursday" instead of the current "T.G.I.F."[4]

Nevertheless, it should be noted that most of the pioneer four-day plans have shortened the workweek but not the worktime. Forty hours has remained the norm, whether divided into five eight-hour days or four ten-hour days. The four-day workweek may be the precursor of a 32-hour workweek, but only if the social invention of the shorter workweek is accompanied by technical inventions which allow the maintenance of production levels.

Perhaps predictably, the prospect of less work and more leisure time has inspired an almost wholly negative reaction among journalistic and other sages who apparently fear that working people will be incapable of finding anything more rewarding to do with their leisure than putting in time in the factory. The old Victorian innocence about tech-nological change has long since been replaced by an invet-erate misgiving. Changes in the ever-changing organiza-tion of work have provided targets for one diatribe after another, some rational, others less so. Charlie Chaplin's film *Modern Times* brilliantly satirized the depersonalizing effect of the assembly line. Aldous Huxley's novel *Brave New World*, depicting a future society in which "the year of our Lord" has become "the year of our Ford," eloquently expressed, despite some logical gaps, a fear that enthroned technology might do away with art and beauty along with pain and suffering.

More flamboyantly, Czechoslovak playwright Karel Capek based his drama *R.U.R.* on an insurrection of robots employed in industry. The word "robot" itself comes from Capek's play, and rebellious robots and seditious androids have filled the pages of science fiction since.

Most recently the apprehension has been expressed by many writers that the individual worker is doomed to deg-radation into a helpless cog in what Lewis Mumford has called the "mega-machine," meaning the vast agglomera-tion of power, machines, and bureaucracy of modern in-dustrial society.[5] French philosopher Jacques Ellul consid-ers that "Modern man's state of mind is completely domi-nated by technical values." Picturing the machine as leading man inexorably into a new "milieu," one that in contrast to our old milieu, nature, is artificial, autonomous, self-determining, nihilistic, and with means taking primacy over ends, Ellul asks if man can ever be really free in a technolog-ical society.[6]

In answer to Mumford, Ellul, and others, it has been pointed out that the problem is not whether man can be-come master of the machine so much as whether man can become master of himself. It is a poor carpenter, in the old adage, who blames his tools. The question, in its varying senses of whether the machine threatens to become the master, will be answered not only by man's capacity to reorganize his work increasingly to his own advantage, but by his ability to define that advantage in increasingly imaginative terms.

Only in very recent years have Capek's robots actually begun to appear in significant numbers in industry. Light-sensitive cells, chemically sensitive materials, solid-state devices, and computers have made possible the construction of robot mechanisms that simulate human locomotion and human sensing, responding to light, sound, heat, and even taste and smell. First found valuable in handling dangerous chemicals and radioactive materials, robots also proved useful for manipulating components in high-temperature, low-temperature, or oxygen-free atmospheres, and in the 1970's began taking on such everyday industrial tasks as spot-welding automobile roofs (and successfully distinguishing among four different models coming down the assembly line in random order). They promised to take over the hardest, dirtiest, and most hazardous jobs, to the satisfaction of labor as well as management.

The intrusion of increasingly sophisticated robots into the workplace is likely to stir a fresh wave of trepidation in some quarters. A robot differs from other automation in that it duplicates human motions and can be programed for a variety of tasks, like a human worker. Robots' freedom from strain and fatigue allow them to outperform human workers at arduous labor, and improvements now foreseen by their manufacturers promise to make them steadily more versatile. Experimental robots have been induced to do rather remarkable things, like learning to play chess, to memorize a maze, or to arrange a set of blocks in a certain order on command. Nevertheless, barring a presently un-foreseeable improvement in computers, the robots of even the twenty-first century will not begin to rival man in the peculiarly human area of judgment or the recognition of significance. "If man can continuously develop his facul-ties," concludes British expert David Foster, "he has nothing to fear from . . . robots."

Instead, this newest chapter in the long-unfolding story of the replacement of human muscles by mechanical con-trivances promises to complete the emancipation of the world's workers from drudgery and danger. One of the most popular technological specters, turned docile and be-neficent, will contribute to what may finally become a virtu-ally nonhuman work force.

As we have seen, the worker of the 1970's, seated at the console of an automated factory, seems to have risen from his old status as slave to become instead an overseer of slave machinery. Perhaps the oncoming army of robots will even-tually reverse the condition man dwelt in throughout the long dawn of prehistory, when he had no word for work because work was synonymous with living. Perhaps in the future he will have no word for work because he no longer needs to do any.

More precisely, he will no longer need to do work in its pejorative sense—the unending, bone-wearying, soul-starving toil of plowing and planting, of lifting and drag-ging, of digging in the mines, of feeding machinery, of fighting the moving assembly line. Instead, he will be free to do the work that a robot cannot do, and which expresses his own humanness—to build, carve, paint, write, act, design, to recover the charm of craftsmanship in an atmosphere of freedom. Is this prospect so alarming?

Notes

CHAPTER 1

[1]Franz Boas, *The Mind of Primitive Man* (New York, Macmillan, 1911).

[2]Christian theology, of course, ascribes the necessity for work to Adam's fall. In the King James translation of the Bible and in the Revised Standard Version, the exact expression is: "In the sweat of thy face shalt thou eat bread, until thou return to the ground. . . ." (Genesis 3:19). The more familiar phrase which forms the title of this book—"by the sweat of thy brow"—was used in varying forms by Cervantes, Sterne, and Thoreau.

[3]Hannah Arendt's distinction between labor ("making a living," usually through employment) and work (a creative effort which provides an artificial world of things) is meaningless in the context of most of human history. Hannah Arendt, *The Human Condition* (Chicago, University of Chicago Press, 1958), pp. 127 ff.

[4]Herbert Spencer, *Principles of Sociology* (New York, D. Appleton, 3 vols., 1901).

[5]Emile Durkheim, *The Division of Labor in Society*, 2nd ed. (New York, Free Press, 1966), p. 41.

[6]Peter F. Drucker, "Work and Tools," *Technology and Culture* 1 (1960), p. 30.

[7]Adam Smith, *An Inquiry into the Nature and Causes of the Wealth of Nations* (New York, Modern Library, 1937), Book I, Chap. 3.

CHAPTER 2

[1]V. Gordon Childe, "Early Forms of Society," in Charles Singer, E. J.

Holmyard, and A. R. Hall, *A History of Technology* (Oxford, Oxford University Press, 5 vols., 1954-58), Vol. I, Chap. 2.

[2]Carleton S. Coon, *The Hunting Peoples* (Boston, Little, Brown, 1971); Richard B. Lee and Irven DeVore, eds., *Man the Hunter* (Chicago, Aldine Publishing Company, 1966); C. Darryl Forde, *Habitat, Economy and Society* (New York, Dutton, 1961).

[3]A. K. Sertel, "The Nature of Power Relations in Hunter-Gatherer Societies," *Hatceppe Bulletin of Social Sciences and Humanities* 1 (1971), pp. 52-70.

[4]Lee and DeVore, *op. cit.*

[5]Claude Lévi-Strauss, *The Raw and the Cooked: Introduction to a Science of Mythology* (New York, Harper and Row, 1969).

[6]Ralph L. Beals in J. H. Steward, ed., *Irrigation Civilizations* (Washington, Pan American Union, 1955), p. 55.

[7]Samuel Lilley, *Men, Machines and History, the Story of Tools and Machines in Relation to Social Progress* (New York, International Publishers, 1966), p. 3.

[8]Gordon Childe, *What Happened in History* (Baltimore, Penguin Books, 1965), Chaps. 3 and 4.

[9]Theodore A. Wertime, "Man's First Encounters with Metallurgy," *Science* 146 (December, 1964), pp. 1257-67.

[10]Nelson Glueck, *The Other Side of the Jordan* (Cambridge, Mass., American School of Oriental Research, 1940).

[11]R. J. Forbes, *Metallurgy in Antiquity* (Leiden, Netherlands, E. J. Brill, 1950).

CHAPTER 3

[1]Karl A. Wittfogel, *Oriental Despotism: A Comparative Study of Total Power* (New Haven, Yale University Press, 1957), p. 18.

[2]Robert McC. Adams, *The Evolution of Urban Societies: Early Mesopotamia and Prehispanic Mexico* (Chicago, Aldine Publishing Co., 1966); William T. Sanders and Barbara J. Price, *Mesoamerica: The Evolution of a Civilization* (New York, Random House, 1968); Frank Hole, "Investigating the Origins of Mesopotamian Civilization," *Science* 153 (August 5, 1966), pp. 605-11.

[3]Gordon Childe, *Man Makes Himself* (New York, Oxford University Press, 1936).

[4]Franz Oppenheimer, *The State* (Indianapolis, Bobbs-Merrill Co., 1914).

[5]Robert L. Carneiro, "A Theory of the Origin of the State," *Science* 169 (August 21, 1970), pp. 733-38.

[6]See Friedrich Engels, *Origin of the Family, Private Property and the State* (New York, International Publishers, 1972); also S. Lilley, *op. cit.*, p. 9.

[7]Xenophon, *Oeconomicus*, IV, 2, 3 (in Xenophon's *Socratic Discourse*, with a new literal translation of the *Oeconomicus* by Carnes Lord. Ithaca, Cornell University Press, 1970).

[8]Aristotle, *Politics* 1329A, 1-2 (in the works of Aristotle, trans. into English under the editorship of W. D. Ross, London, Oxford University Press, 1952-65).

[9]*Plutarch's Lives* (New York, Modern Library, 1932 ed.), p. 183.

[10]Cicero, *De Officiis*, I, 42 (English trans. by Walter Miller, Cambridge, Mass., Harvard University Press, 1961).

[11]Claude Mossé, *The Ancient World at Work* (London, Chatto and Windus, 1969), pp. 27-28.

[12]Edmund Burke, attacking the French Revolution in 1789, pronounced manual laborers unfit to participate in government, and in a footnote added to his speech (see Thomas H. D. Mahoney, ed., *Reflections on the Revolution in France* [1955]), quoted Ecclesiasticus: "How can he get wisdom that holdeth the plow, and that glorieth in the good; that driveth oxen; and is occupied in their labors, and whose talk is of bullocks?" A justification for slavery offered by plantation owners of the antebellum (U.S.) South was that it freed the elite for cultural pursuits, including the development of democratic political institutions.

[13]Quoted in Gustave Glotz, *Ancient Greece at Work* (London, Routledge and Paul, 1927), p. 222.

[14]Classic statements of this position are to be found in Benjamin Farrington, *Greek Science*, 2 vols. (New York, Penguin Books, 1944); S. Lilley, *op. cit.*, pp. 39-40; Childe, *What Happened in History*, p. 258. Not everyone agrees with this interpretation: see A. G. Drachmann, "The Classical Civilizations," in Melvin Kranzberg and Carroll W. Pursell, Jr., eds., *Technology in Western Civilization*, 2 vols. (New York, Oxford University Press, 1967), Vol. I, Chap. 4; and S. C. Gilfillan, "The Inventive Lag in Classical Mediterranean Society," *Technology and Culture* 3 (1962), p. 85.

CHAPTER 4

[1]E. M. Jope, "Agricultural Implements," in Singer, *History of Technology*, Vol. 2, p. 92.

[2]Matthew 13:8

[3] According to G. E. Fussell, "Farming Systems of the Classical Era," *Technology and Culture* 8 (1967), pp. 16-44, a Greek peasant of Hesiod's day with a wife and two children would probably sow six acres of land (leaving six fallow) in order to raise thirty bushels of grain, enough to support the family for a year.

[4] Also known as *De re rustica*, ca. 160 B.C.

[5] Fussell, *loc. cit.*

[6] See Glotz, *op. cit.*, pp. 129, 378-79; Mossé, *op. cit.*, pp. 20-21.

CHAPTER 5

[1] The best account of ancient crafts is to be found in Carl Roebuck, ed., *The Muses at Work: Arts, Crafts and Professions in Ancient Greece and Rome* (Cambridge, Mass., MIT Press, 1969). Still useful is Albert Neuberger, *The Technical Arts and Sciences of the Ancients* (London, Methuen, 1930).

[2] Xenophon, *Cyropaedia*, VIII, 2, 5 (with English trans., Cambridge, Mass., Harvard University Press, 1960-1).

[3] Arthur Lane, *Greek Pottery* (London, Farber and Farber, 1963).

[4] Gisela M. A. Richter, *The Furniture of the Greeks, Etruscans and Romans* (London, Phaidon Press, 1966).

[5] See Glotz, *op. cit.*, pp. 323 ff.

[6] See Sir Lindsay Scott, "Pottery," in Singer, *History of Technology*, Vol. 1, Chap. 15; also Gisela M. A. Richter, *Craft of Athenian Pottery* (1923).

[7] R. J. Forbes, *Studies in Ancient Technology* (London, E. J. Brill, 1956), Vol. 4.

[8] H. Ling Roth, *Studies in Primitive Looms* (Halifax, England, I. King & Sons Ltd., 1934).

[9] For a full description of the operations of the wool industry at Pompeii, see Walter O. Moeller, "The *Lanfricarius* and the *Officinae Lanifricariae* at Pompeii," *Technology and Culture* 7 (Fall 1966), pp. 493-96.

[10] Friedrich Klemm, *A History of Western Technology* (London, Allen and Unwin, 1959), p. 28.

[11] G. M. Calhoun, "Ancient Athenian Mining," *Journal of Economic and Business History* 35 (1931), pp. 333 ff.

CHAPTER 6

[1] See Ahmed Fakhry, *The Pyramids* (Chicago, University of Chicago Press, 1961), for the most complete account of pyramid building.

[2]I. E. S. Edwards, *The Pyramids of Egypt* (Baltimore, Penguin Books, 1961), p. 262.

[3]C. St. C. Davison, "Transporting Sixty-ton Statues in Early Assyria and Egypt," *Technology and Culture* 2 (1961), pp. 11-16.

[4]See L. Sprague de Camp, *The Ancient Engineers* (Garden City, N.Y., Doubleday, 1963), Chaps. 6-7; A. G. Drachmann, *loc. cit.*

CHAPTER 7

[1]The Muslim geographer Ibn-Khurdadbih, a provincial postmaster of Persia, described the activities of the Radanites: "These merchants speak Arabic, Persian, Roman, the languages of the Franks, Andalusians and Slavs. They journey from west to east, from east to west, partly on land, partly by sea. They transport from the west eunuchs, female and male slaves, silk, castor, marten and other furs, and swords. They take ship in the land of the Franks, on the Western Sea [Mediterranean] and steer for Farama [Egypt]. There they load their goods on the backs of camels and go by land to Qulzum [Suez] . . . They embark in the East [Red] Sea and sail to al-Jar and Jeddah [in Arabia]; they go on to Sind [between Persia and India], India and China. On their return they carry musk, aloes, camphor, cinnamon and other products of the Eastern countries." Howard Adelson, *Medieval Commerce* (Princeton, D. Van Nostrand Co., 1962), pp. 127-8. An account of the Radanites may be found in L. Rabinowitz, *Jewish Merchant Adventurers, A Study of the Radanites* (London, E. Goldston, 1948).

[2]Bloch cites the history of the mill as a test case. "The more effective use of animal motive-power and the harnessing of water-power were developments that took place simultaneously, for the very good reason that they originated in the same need. Was the decline of slavery then a result of this? By no means: it was much more probably a cause, leading on to a technical revolution. . . ." Marc Bloch, *Land and Work in Medieval Europe* (New York, Harper & Row, 1967), pp. 176-82.

[3]H. S. Bettenson, ed., *Documents of the Christian Church*, 2nd ed. (London and New York, Oxford University Press, 1966).

[4]G. C. Homans, *English Villagers of the Thirteenth Century* (New York, Russell & Russell, 1960), pp. 45-46, believes in the reality of the eight-ox team and suggests that the pictorial evidence is not realistic—"It would be hard to crowd eight oxen into the margin [of a manuscript]." He also suggests that the eight-ox team may have been divided into two sets, working on alternate days; that the ill-fed cattle of the Middle Ages may

have been weak and small, so that eight were needed to plow; or that plowing with eight oxen was the result of the iron weight of medieval custom. Homans' reasoning seems unsatisfactory to most historians, who lean to the theory that the eight-ox team was a legal concept.

[5]For a comprehensive discussion of medieval technology and its effects, see Lynn White, *Medieval Technology and Social Change* (Oxford, Clarendon Press, 1962); also "Technology in the Middle Ages," in Kranzberg and Pursell, *Technology in Western Civilization*, Vol. I, pp. 66-79.

[6]"Champion country" (*champagne*) can be seen today in France, *e.g.*, in the regions around Chartres and Reims, where the land lies in broad open stretches of arable fields, broken only by stands of trees and an occasional village, contrasted with the "woodland country" (*bocage*) of western Normandy, where small fields are surrounded by ditches, hedges, and earthen or stone walls. Speculation about the origin of the two types of cultivation has centered around soil types and racial-cultural origins, champion country roughly coinciding with light filterable soil and Germanic settlement, woodland with heavy water-holding soil and Celtic settlement. For an extended discussion, see G. C. Homans, *English Villagers of the Thirteenth Century*; also his "The Rural Sociology of Medieval England," *Past and Present* (1953), pp. 32-43. A detailed description of the organization of work in open-field (champion) country can be found in H. S. Bennett, *Life on the English Manor* (Cambridge, Cambridge University Press, 1960).

[7]W. W. Skeat, ed., *Piers Plowman*; William Langland, *The Vision of William Concerning Piers the Plowman* (New York, Cooper Square, 1886).

[8]Frederick Furnivall, ed., Robert Mannyng of Brunne, *Handlyng Synne* (London, K. Paul, French Trübner & Co. Ltd., for the Early English Text Society, 1901, 1903).

[9]Quoted in W. O. Ault, "Some Early Village By-Laws," *English Historical Review* (1930).

[10]Lionel Casson, *Ships and Seamanship in the Ancient World* (Princeton, N.J., Princeton University Press, 1971).

[11]Lynn White, Jr., "What Accelerated Technological Progress in the Western Middle Ages?" in A. C. Crombie, ed., *Scientific Change* (London, Heinemann, 1963), pp. 272-91.

CHAPTER 8

[1]The guilds listed are from the tax list preserved from 1292, cited by

Joseph and Francis Gries in *Life in a Medieval City,* (New York, Thomas Y. Crowell, 1969).

[2] For an account of the medieval woolen industry, see Eleanor M. Carus-Wilson, "The Woolen Industry," in M. M. Postan and E. E. Rich, eds., *Cambridge Economic History*, Vol. II, *Trade in the Middle Ages* (Cambridge, Cambridge University Press, 1952).

[3] For a detailed description of the business operation of a Flemish wool entrepreneur under the putting-out system, see Joseph and Frances Gies, *Merchants and Moneymen* (New York, Thomas Y. Crowell Co., 1972), Chap. 8, "A Flemish Merchant Prince," pp. 89-97.

[4] For an account of an Italian merchant company of the Calimala Guild, see "The Calimala Guild: The Alberti Company of Florence," in *Merchants and Moneymen, op. cit.*

[5] Pierre Boissonade, *Life and Work in Medieval Europe (Fifth to Fifteenth Centuries)* (New York, Harper & Row, 1964).

[6] Lynn White, Jr., "Medieval Roots of Modern Technology," in *Perspectives in Medieval History* (Chicago, University of Chicago Press, 1963).

[7] *Ibid.*

CHAPTER 9

[1] The once-popular notion that Gothic architecture was created by anonymous craftsmen has long since been exploded by scholars. In 1920 the *Révue archéologique* published the names of over 500 architect-engineers in France alone, and in 1954 John Harvey published a dictionary of English medieval architects. Altogether the names of at least 25,000 master masons and others who worked on the Gothic cathedrals are known.

[2] John H. Harvey, *English Medieval Architects* (London, Batsford, 1954); John Fitchen, *The Construction of Gothic Cathedrals* (Oxford, Clarendon Press, 1961).

[3] The sketchbook of Villard de Honnecourt, thirteenth-century architect-engineer, contains numerous drawings not only of structural but decorative elements, and of machinery, such as a mechanical saw for splitting beams. See T. Bowie, ed., *Sketchbook of Villard de Honnecourt* (Bloomington, Ind., Indiana University Press, 1959, p. 58.

[4] Agricola's classic exists in an English translation thanks to a former president of the United States, Herbert Hoover, and his wife Lou H. Hoover. The Hoover translation appeared in a limited edition in 1912, and in a trade edition in 1950. See also Bern Dibner, *Agricola on Metals* (Norwalk, Conn., Burndy Library, 1958).

CHAPTER 10

[1]George Unwin, *Industrial Organization in the Sixteenth and Seventeenth Centuries* (Oxford, Clarendon Press, 1904).

[2]See C. Wright Mills, *White Collar: The American Middle Class* (New York, Oxford University Press, 1951), pp. 215-23; R. H. Tawney, *Religion and the Rise of Capitalism* (London, John Murray, 1926; (New York, New American Library, 1955).

[3]G. E. Fussell, *The Farmer's Tools, 1500-1900* (London, A. Melrose, 1952); B. H. Slicher von Bath, *The Agrarian History of Western Europe* (London, E. Arnold, 1963).

[4]Paul Mantoux, *The Industrial Revolution in the Eighteenth Century* (revised ed., London, J. Cape, 1961), Chap. 1.

[5]Herbert Heaton, *History of the Yorkshire Woolen and Worsted Industries* (Oxford, Clarendon Press, 1920).

[6]See Unwin, *op. cit.*

[7]Charles W. Cole, *Colbert and a Century of French Mercantilism* (2 vols., New York, Columbia University Press, 1939).

[8]E. L. J. Coornaert, "European Economic Institutions and the New World; the Chartered Companies," in E. E. Rich and C. H. Wilson, eds., *The Cambridge Economic History of Europe* (Cambridge, Cambridge University Press), Vol. 4, *The Economy of Expanding Europe in the Sixteenth and Seventeenth Centuries*, Chap. 4.

[9]E. E. Rich, "Colonial Settlement and Its Labour Problems," *Cambridge Economic History of Europe*, Vol. 4, Chap. 6.

CHAPTER 11

[1]Abbott Payson Usher, "The Textile Industry, 1750-1830," in Kranzberg and Pursell, *op. cit.*, Vol. 1, Chap. 14.

[2]Andrew Ure, *Philosophy of Manufactures* (London, C. Knight, 1835), p. 14.

[3]Adam Smith, *op. cit.*, Book I, Chap. 1.

[4]W. Ranger, in *Report on . . . Halifax* (1851), cited in E. P. Thompson, *The Making of the English Working Class* (Harmondsworth, Penguin Books, 1968) or (London, V. Gollcz, 1963), calculated the average age at death of "gentry manufacturers and their families" at fifty-five; shopkeepers, twenty-four; mill operatives, twenty-two. Thompson admits that the evidence is not statistically conclusive, but cites as additional support the testimony of Dr. Holland of Sheffield: "We have no hesitation in asserting, that the sufferings of the working classes, and consequently the rate of mortality, are greater now than in former times.

Indeed, in most manufacturing districts the rate of mortality in these classes is appalling to contemplate, when it can be studied in reference to them alone, *and not in connection with the entire population.* The supposed gain on the side of longevity arises chiefly from . . . a relatively much more numerous middle class than formerly existed."

⁵G. Sturt, *The Wheelwright's Shop* (Cambridge, Eng., Cambridge University Press, 1963), Chaps. X and XXXVII. Sturt also gives a revealing picture of the craft pride of his wheelwright employees: "They possibly (and properly) exaggerated the respect for good workmanship and material . . . it happened not infrequently that a disgusted workman would refuse to use what I had supplied to him" because a wheel made of inferior wood would not measure up to "what good wheelwright's work should be like."

⁶Neil J. Smelser, *Social Change in the Industrial Revolution* (Chicago, University of Chicago Press, 1959).

⁷Neil McKendrick, "Josiah Wedgwood and Factory Discipline," *Historical Journal* 4 (1961), pp. 30-55.

⁸Quoted in Thompson, *The Making of the English Working Class,* from V. W. Bladen, "The Potteries in the Industrial Revolution," *Economics Journal* 1 (Supplement, 1926-29), p. 130.

⁹J. Smith, *Memoirs of Wool* (1747), II, p. 308. Quoted in Thompson, *The Making of the English Working Class.*

¹⁰Great Britain, *Sessional Papers,* 1833, Vol. 123.

¹¹E. J. Hobsbawm, *Labouring Men* (London, Weidenfeld & Nicolson, 1964).

¹²Smith, *The Wealth of Nations,* Book 1, Chap. 1.

¹³Hobsbawm, *op. cit.,* Chap. 2; Thompson, *op. cit.,* Chap. 14.

¹⁴Quoted in Thompson, *The Making of the English Working Class,* p. 199.

CHAPTER 12

¹See John B. Rae, "The Rationalization of Production," in Kranzberg and Pursell, *Technology in Western Civilization,* Vol. 2, p. 37.

²Scott Buchanan, "Technology as a System of Exploitation," in Carl F. Stover, ed., *The Technological Order* (Detroit, Michigan, Wayne State University Press, 1963), p. 156.

³See Eugene S. Ferguson, "Metallurgical and Machine-Tool Developments," in Kranzberg and Pursell, *Technology in Western Civilization,* Vol. 1, Chap. 16; Carroll W. Pursell, Jr., "Machines and Machine Tools, 1830-1880," *ibid.,* Chap. 23.

[4]Robert S. Woodbury, *History of the Lathe to 1850* (Cambridge, Mass., MIT Press, 1961).

[5]A British mission to the United States in 1853 decided that "the real secret of American productivity is that American society is imbued through and through with the desirability, the rightness, the morality of production. Men serve God in America, in all seriousness and sincerity, through striving for economic efficiency." Quoted by Charles L. Sanford, "The Intellectual Origins and New Worldliness of American Industry," *Journal of Economic History*, 18 (1958), p. 16, and cited by Lynn White, Jr., in "Technology Assessment From the Stance of a Medieval Historian," *American Historical Review* (1974). For a comparison of British and American technological differences, see H. J. Habakkuk, *American and British Technology in the Nineteenth Century: The Search for Labour-Saving Inventions* (Cambridge, England, Cambridge University Press, 1962).

[6]David J. Jeremy, "Innovation in American Textile Technology During the Early 19th Century," *Technology and Culture*, 14 (1973), pp. 40-76.

[7]Nathan Rosenberg, ed., *The American System of Manufactures* (Edinburgh, Edinburgh University Press, 1969).

[8]Robert S. Woodbury, "The Legend of Eli Whitney and Interchangeable Parts," *Technology and Culture* 1 (1960), pp. 235-53.

[9]Merritt Roe Smith, "John H. Hall, Simeon North, and the Milling Machine: The Nature of Innovation Among Antebellum Arms Makers," *Technology and Culture* 14 (1973), pp. 573-91.

[10]Mrs. Wilfred C. Leland and Minnie Dubbs Millbrook, *Master of Precision: Henry M. Leland* (Detroit, Michigan, Wayne State University Press, 1966).

CHAPTER 13

[1]F. L. Lane, *Venetian Ships and Shipbuilders of the Renaissance* (Baltimore, Johns Hopkins Press, 1934).

[2]Greville and Dorothy Bathe, *Oliver Evans: A Chronicle of Early American Engineering* (Philadelphia, Pa., The Historical Society of Pennsylvania, 1935).

[3]See Jeremy, *loc. cit.*

[4]Siegfried Giedion, *Mechanization Takes Command* (New York, Oxford University Press, 1948).

[5]Allan Nevins and Frank E. Hill, *Ford, The Times, The Man, The Company*, Vol. I (New York, Scribners, 1954); Roger Burlingame, *Henry Ford: A Great Life in Brief* (1955); John B. Rae, *American Automobile Manu-*

facturers: The First Forty Years (Philadelphia, Pa., Chelton Co. Book Division, 1959).

[6]Glenn A. Niemeyer, *The Automotive Career of Ransom E. Olds* (East Lansing, Mich., Michigan State University Bureau of Business and Economic Research, 1963).

[7]Rae, "The Rationalization of Production," in Kranzberg and Pursell, *op. cit.*, Vol. 2, pp. 44-47.

[8]Georges Friedmann, *The Anatomy of Work* (Glencoe, Illinois, Free Press, 1961).

[9]Alexis de Tocqueville, *Democracy in America* (New York, G. Adlond, 1839), Vol. 2, pp. 158 ff.

[10]John Ruskin, "The Nature of Gothic," in *The Stones of Venice* (London, Allen & Unwin, 1925).

[11]T. E. Bottomore and M. Rubel, eds., *Karl Marx: Selected Writings in Sociology and Social Philosophy* (1964).

[12]Thorstein Veblen, *The Instinct of Workmanship and the State of Industrial Art* (New York, Macmillan, 1914).

CHAPTER 14

[1]Herbert G. Gutman quotes the passage, originally written by a New York ship carpenter for *Knight's Penny Magazine* in 1846, in "Work, Culture and Society in Industrializing America, 1815-1919," *American Historial Review* (1973).

[2]From Franklin E. Coyne, *The Development of the Cooperage Industry in the United States* (Chicago, Lumber Buyers Publishing Co., 1940), quoted in Gutman, *loc cit.*

[3]Ure, *op. cit.*, p. 423.

[4]Robert L. Heilbroner, "Do Machines Make History?" *Technology and Culture* 8 (1967), p. 341.

[5]Peter F. Drucker, *Management: Tasks, Responsibility and Practice* (New York, Harper & Row, 1974).

[6]Theodore Caplow, *The Sociology of Work* (New York, McGraw Hill, 1954); Edward Gross, *Work and Society* (New York, Thomas Y. Crowell, 1958).

[7]Lewis Mumford, *Technics and Civilization* (New York, Harcourt, Brace, 1934), Chap. 5.

[8]Smith, *The Wealth of Nations*, Book 1.

[9]Goldwin Smith, *Lectures on the Study of History* (New York, Harper & Bros., 1866), pp. 32-33.

[10] Georges Friedmann, *op. cit.*, pp. x., 92.

CHAPTER 15

[1] See Georg Borgstrom, "Food and Agriculture in the Nineteenth Century," in Kranzberg and Pursell, *Technology in Western Civilization*, I, Chap. 24; Paul W. Gates, *The Farmer's Age: Agriculture, 1815-1860* (New York, Holt, Rinehart & Winston, 1960); and Fred A. Shannon, *The Farmer's Last Frontier, 1860-97* (New York, Farrar & Rinehart, 1945).

[2] Stewart Holbrook, *Machines of Plenty: Pioneering in American Agriculture* (New York, Macmillan, 1955).

[3] For twentieth-century developments in food and agricultural technology, see Kranzberg and Pursell, *Technology in Western Civilization*, Vol. II, Part 7, with chapters by Wayne D. Rasmussen, Reynold M. Wik, Aaron J. Ihde, and Georg Borgstrom.

[4] Reynold M. Wik, "Science and American Agriculture," in David D. van Tassel and Michael G. Hall, eds., *Science and Society in the United States* (Homewood, Ill., Dorsey Press, 1966), pp. 81-106; T. Swann Harding, *Two Blades of Grass: A History of Scientific Development in the U.S. Department of Agriculture* (Norman, Oklahoma, University of Oklahoma Press, 1947).

[5] See the annual *Yearbooks* of the United States Department of Agriculture.

[6] Wayne D. Rasmussen, "Advances in American Agriculture: The Mechanical Tomato Harvester as a Case Study," *Technology and Culture* 9 (1968), pp. 531-43.

[7] Folke Dovring, "Soviet Farm Mechanization in Perspective," *Slavic Review* 25 (1966), pp. 287-302.

[8] V.W. Ruttan and Yujiro Hayami, "Technology Transfer and Agricultural Development," *Technology and Culture* 14 (1973), pp. 119-51.

CHAPTER 16

[1] *Encyclopaedia Britannica*, 13th edition.

[2] The standard biography of Taylor is Frank Barkley Copley, *Frederick Winslow Taylor* (2 vols., New York, Harper & Bros., 1923); see also Sudhir Kakar, *Frederick Taylor: A Study in Personality and Innovation* (Cambridge, Mass, MIT Press, 1971).

[3] Taylor's major ideas are best conveyed in his *The Principles of Scientific Management* (New York & London, Harper & Bros., 1911); a wider range of his comments are collected in *Scientific Management: Comprising Shop*

Management, The Principles of Scientific Management Testimony Before the House Special Committee (1947).

[4]Quoted in Robert H. Guest, "The Rationalization of Management," in Kranzberg and Pursell, *Technology in Western Civilization*, Vol. 2, Chap. 5.

[5]"Hearings before the Special Committee of the House of Representatives to Investigate the Taylor and Other Systems of Shop Management, under the Authority of House Resolution 90" (1912), III, pp. 1377-1508.

[6]Henri Fayol, *General and Industrial Management* (London, Pittman, 1949).

[7]See L. P. Alford, *Henry Laurence Gantt: Leader in Industry* (1934), and Edna Yost, Frank and Lillian Gilbreth, *Partners for Life* (New Brunswick, N.J., Rutgers University Press, 1949).

[8]See Charles R. Walker, "The Social Effects of Mass Production," in Kranzberg and Pursell, *Technology in Western Civilization*, Vol. 2, pp. 93-94.

[9]See Samuel Haber, *Efficiency and Uplift: Scientific Management in the Progressive Era, 1890-1920* (Chicago, Illinois, University of Chicago Press, 1964), and Edwin T. Layton, Jr., *The Revolt of the Engineers: Social Responsibility and the American Engineering Profession* (Cleveland, Ohio, Press of Case Western Reserve University, 1971).

[10]Quoted in Daniel J. Boorstin, *The Democratic Experience* (New York, Random House, 1973), Chap. 41.

[11]Nicos P. Mouzelis, in *Organization and Bureaucracy, an Analysis of Modern Theories* (Chicago, Illinois, Aldine Publishing Co., 1968), pp. 81-87, uses the term "technicist bias" in describing Taylor's attempt to "apply his method in order to solve problems the handling of which demand a more inclusive conceptual framework." He goes on to argue that Taylor was guilty of "a misconception of the nature of scientific method," pointing out that even "if it is scientifically possible to determine the length of time in which a certain job could be done . . . there is no scientific way of determining the time in which a certain job ought to be done."

[12]C. R. Walker and R. H. Guest, *The Man on the Assembly Line* (Cambridge, Mass., Harvard University Press, 1952).

[13]This did not prevent Lenin from becoming an enthusiastic advocate of Taylorism. In an article in *Pravda* in 1918 he urged "the study and teaching of the Taylor system and its systematic trial and adoption." (Cited in Daniel Bell, "Frederick W. Taylor on Scientific Management," in *An American Primer*, ed. by Daniel J. Boorstin, p. 749.) (Chicago, Illinois, University of Chicago Press, 1966).

CHAPTER 17

[1]Mayo also published general studies on this question: *The Human Problems of Industrial Civilization* (New York, Macmillan, 1933) and *The Social Problems of Industrial Civilization* (Boston-Division of Research, Graduate School of Business Ad., Harvard University, 1945).

[2]Warner's *The Social System of the Modern Factory* (New Haven, Yale University Press, 1947) used the basic approach developed in the Hawthorne studies but carried it into community-industry relations, showing how large environmental changes link with individual behavior and can affect union organization, strikes, etc.

[3]See L. Coch and J. R. P. French, Jr., "Overcoming Resistance to Change," *Human Relations* (1948), pp. 512-32.

[4]See D. Katz, *et al.*, *Productivity, Supervision and Morale Among Railroad Workers* (Ann Arbor, Michigan, Survey Research Center, University of Michigan, 1951).

[5]E. L. Trist, *et al.*, *Organizational Choice* (London, Tavistock Publications, 1963).

[6]See, for example, Ernest J. McCormick, *Human Factors Engineering*, 3rd ed. (New York, McGraw-Hill, 1970).

CHAPTER 18

[1]See James R. Bright, "The Development of Automation," in Kranzberg and Pursell, *Technology in Western Civilization*, Vol. 2, Chap. 41.

[2]Otto Mayr, *The Origins of Feedback Control* (Cambridge, Mass., MIT Press, 1970).

[3]Thomas M. Smith, "Origins of the Computer," in Kranzberg and Pursell, *Technology in Western Civilization*, Vol. 2, Chap. 20.

[4]*Technology and the American Economy*, Report of the National Commission on Technology, Automation, and Economic Progress (6 vols., Washington, Government Printing Office, 1966).

[5]Norbert Wiener, *The Human Use of Human Beings* (Boston, Houghton Mifflin, 1950), and *Cybernetics* (Cambridge, Mass., MIT Press, 1948).

[6]See John Diebold, *Automation—The Advent of the Automatic Factory* (New York, Van Nostrand, 1952); John T. Dunlop, ed., *Automation and Technological Change* (Englewood Cliffs, N.J., Prentice Hall, 1962); Herbert A. Simon, *The Shape of Automation* (New York, Harper & Row, 1965).

[7]Ida R. Hoos, *Automation in the Office* (Washington, Public Affairs Press, 1961).

[8]William W. Brickman and Stanley Lehrer, eds., *Automation, Education, and Human Values* (New York, School & Society Books, 1966).

[9]Charles E. Silberman and the Editors of Fortune, *The Myths of Automation* (New York, Harper & Row, 1966).

CHAPTER 19

[1]*Cybernetics,* op. cit.

[2]*Moscow News,* March 31, 1973.

[3]Peter F. Drucker, *The Age of Discontinuity: Guidelines to Our Changing Society* (New York, Harper & Row, 1969).

[4]Edward Ames and Nathan Rosenberg, "The Progressive Division and Specialization of Industries," *Journal of Development Studies* 1 (1964-65), pp. 367-72.

[5]Walker and Guest, *Man on the Assembly Line,* pp. 84-85.

[6]Sebastian de Grazia, *Of Time, Work, and Leisure* (New York, Twentieth Century Fund, 1962).

[7]Charles R. DeCarlo "Perspectives on Technology," in Eli Ginzberg, ed., *Technology and Social Change* (New York, Columbia University Press, 1964), pp. 8-37.

[8]The interview originally appeared in *Personnel,* a publication of the American Management Association, and was reprinted with permission in "The Rationalization of Management," by Robert H. Guest, in Kranzberg and Pursell, *Technology in Western Civilization,* Vol. 2, pp. 55-60. The anonymous worker articulates the assembly line's tyranny perhaps even better than the trained writers:

> On a few jobs I know some fellows can work like hell up the line, then coast. Most jobs you can't do that. If I get ahead maybe ten seconds the next model has more welds to it, so it takes ten seconds extra.... When you get too far behind, you get in a hole—that's what we call it. All hell breaks loose. I get in the next guy's way. The foreman gets sore and they have to rush in a relief man to bail you out.
>
> It's easy for them time-study fellows to come down there with a stopwatch and figure out just how much a man can do in a minute and fifty-two seconds. ... But they can't clock how a man feels from one day to the next. Those guys ought to work on the line for a few weeks and maybe they'll feel some things that they never pick up on the stop watch. . . .

We sometimes kid about it and say we don't need no foreman. That line is the foreman. Some joke.

[9]Quoted in Stanley Parker, *The Future of Work and Leisure* (London, MacGibbon & Kee, 1971), p. 48.

[10]"The Changing Success Ethic," reported in New York *Times*, June 3, 1973.

CHAPTER 20

[1]Bernard J. Muller-Thym, "The Meaning of Automation," *Management Review* (1963).

[2]Address by James E. Webb at Graduation Exercises of Advanced Management Program, Harvard University Graduate School of Business Administration, December 9, 1966.

[3]"Testing the 4-Day Workweek," New York *Times*, July 8, 1973.

[4]Donald Scott, *The Psychology of Work* (London, Duckworth, 1970), p. 188.

[5]William J. Paul, Jr., Keith B. Robertson, and Frederick Herzberg, "Job Enrichment Pays off," *Harvard Business Review* (March-April, 1969), pp. 61-78.

[6]Frederick Herzberg, *Work and the Nature of Man* (Cleveland, Ohio, World Publishing Company, 1966).

[7]John R. Maher, ed., *New Perspectives in Job Enrichment* (New York, Van Nostrand Reinhold, 1971).

[8]Marco Gilliam, "They Really Want to Do a Good Job if We'll Let 'em. . . . ," *Bell Telephone Magazine* (Jan./Feb., 1971), pp. 1-9.

[9]See also Abegglen's earlier study: *The Japanese Factory: Aspects of Its Social Organization* (Glencoe, Illinois, Free Press, 1958).

[10]"Fiat's Social Program Rolling," New York *Times*, June 10, 1973.

[11]Leonard Silk, "On-the-Job Democracy," *International Herald-Tribune*, July 6, 1973.

[12]*Time*, Feb. 12, 1973.

[13]David Riesman, "Leisure and Work in Post-Industrial Society," in Eric Larrabee and R. Meyersohn, eds., *Mass Leisure* (Glencoe, Illinois, Free Press, 1958).

[14]David Jenkins, *Job Power: Blue and White Collar Democracy* (New York, Doubleday, 1973).

CHAPTER 21

[1]Durkheim, *op. cit.*, p. 406.

[2]Daniel Bell, *The Coming of Post-Industrial Society: A Venture in Social*

Forecasting (New York, Basic Books, 1973).

[3]Robert Blauner, *Alienation and Freedom: The Factory Worker and His Industry* (Chicago, Illinois, University of Chicago Press, 1964).

[4]L. Erick Kanter, "Thank God It's Thursday!" in Riva Poor, ed., *4 Days, 40 Hours and Other Forms of the Rearranged Workweek* (New York, New American Library, 1973), pp. 63-68.

[5]Lewis Mumford, *The Myth of the Machine* (New York, Harcourt, Brace, Jovanovich, 1967).

[6]Jacques Ellul, *The Technological Society* (New York, Alfred A. Knopf, 1964).

Index

Abacus, 174
Abegglen, James G., 207
Absenteeism, reduced, with shorter workweek, 202–3
Adaptability, worker, premium on, with increased automation, 189–90
Adding machine, first mechanical, 174–75
Age, and division of labor in prehistory, 14
Agribusiness, 140
Agricola, Georgius, 77–78
Agricultural research, 142
Agricultural surpluses, 23, 24, 26, 60
Agricultural technology
    ancient, 37–38
    in Dark Ages, 59–60
    in 15th to 18th century, 80
Agricultural yields, in mass production farming, 142
Agriculture. *See also* Agricultural technology; Farming
    ancient, 32–38
    European, and discovery of New World, 85–86
    mass production applied to, 139–48
    medieval, low productivity of, 74
    modern
        in Japan, 147
        in Soviet Union, 146–48
        U.S. capital investment in, 142, 145–46
Aiken, Howard, 174
Alienation, worker, 6, 123–24, 193–96; modern management of, 197–211
Alienation and Freedom (Blauner), 213–14
America, discovery of, and effect on European economy, 85
American Management Association, 195
"American system" of manufacturers, 111 ff.

Ames, Edward, 187
"Analytical Engine," 175
Animal mill, 72
Animals
    domestication of, 16
    power use of, on farms, 140
Anomie, and worker, 6, 193, 201, 204; and management personnel, 195
Apprentice craftsmen, 67–68
Aristotle, on necessity of leisure, 28
Arkwright, Richard, 91
Arms industry, ancient specialization in, 46–47
Arte de Calimola, 70
Assembly line, 114, 116–25, 151
    alienation of workers on, 123–24
    automated, 176
    disassembling, in modern industry, 207
    early examples of, 116–18
    in food-processing industry, 142
    and organization of farm work, 142–48
    psychological effects of working on, 191–92
    and Taylorism, 160 Assyrians, 116
Automated industrial system, elements of, 176
Automatic controls, development of, 172–74
Automation, 6, 214–15
    advantages of, 188–89
    basic elements of, 171–72
    developments leading toward, 172–74
    disadvantages of, 189–90
    general impact of, 180, 182–96
    high cost of, 178
    impact on production, 177–81
    and increased consumption, 184
    logic of, 171–81
    psychological difficulties caused by, 190–96
    unemployment and, 183–84
    worker's role in, 178

236